Contents

Section C   Connecting your speech

Section D   RP rhythm

Section E   Practice exercises

Section F   Appendices

Collins

Work on your
Accent

Helen Ashton & Sarah Shepherd

Collins

HarperCollins Publishers
The News Building
1 London Bridge Street
London
SE1 9GF

First edition 2012

10 9 8 7 6 5 4

© HarperCollins Publishers 2012

ISBN 978-0-00-746291-9

Typeset in India by Aptara

Printed in China by RR Donnelley APS

About the authors

Helen Ashton and **Sarah Shepherd** are highly regarded freelance accent and dialect coaches with substantial experience working with students from all around the world. Having trained professionally at London's influential Central School of Speech and Drama, they now teach both actors and non-native speakers of English how to speak with different accents.

How to use this book

Welcome to *Work on your Accent*!

This is a practical workbook to help you work on your English pronunciation. You will be guided through all of the speech sounds of British English and told how to practise further.

It's taken you your whole life so far to talk the way you do, so changing your accent isn't going to be an overnight process. Try to spend a few minutes a day working through a page or two at a time. Accent softening can be tiring so don't try and push through the whole book in one sitting. A little every day or two is plenty!

Most important of all: you will get back what you put in. Accent work is like exercise – the more you do, the fitter you become; the less you do, the harder it feels when you finally hit the gym again.

If you practise regularly, you will change your speech habits faster. If you don't, you won't. It's simple, really.

You can use *Work on your Accent:*

- as a self-study course
- with a teacher in the classroom.

The book has 52 units, each introducing a new sound, or another aspect of pronunciation. Every unit contains explanations and exercises. You will learn to create each sound, and then you will practise each sound in context.

Here is a sample 'Section B' unit, to show you how each one works:

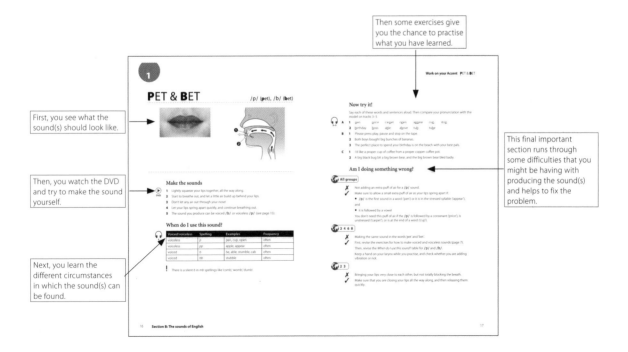

Then some exercises give you the chance to practise what you have learned.

First, you see what the sound(s) should look like.

Then, you watch the DVD and try to make the sound yourself.

Next, you learn the different circumstances in which the sound(s) can be found.

This final important section runs through some difficulties that you might be having with producing the sound(s) and helps to fix the problem.

Before you start

You will be eager to jump in to the sounds – after all, that is why you bought this book! But we highly recommend that you take the time to read the few pages of introductions to the anatomy of speech, mirror practice, RP and IPA (Section A). You will get much more from your hard work if you know the most effective way to study.

More than just sounds

There is more to good pronunciation than just learning the sounds. Alongside studying each sound (in Section B) this book also looks at two other extremely important areas: connecting your speech (Section C) and stress and intonation (Section D). Be sure to spend a good deal of time on these sections – without them, your learning is incomplete.

Extra exercises

At the end of the book in Section E, you will find lots more activities to help you perfect the more difficult sounds.

Using the DVD-ROM

This book comes with a DVD-ROM which you should use to make sure that you are creating each sound correctly. On the DVD-ROM you will find a button to download all of the audio tracks onto your computer. Then you can transfer them to an MP3 player for easy access.

Whenever you can, you should also use the DVD-ROM to watch the video clip for each sound. The videos will help you to see what the sounds should look like when you create them. If you are working by yourself (without a teacher), it is very important that you use these video clips.

DVD

Watch

When you see this symbol, it means that there is a video that you should watch if you can.

Listen

When you see this symbol, it means that you should listen to an audio track.

Language groups

We have divided the world's languages into groups in order to help you know which errors *you* are most likely to make. When you see this symbol, it means we are referring to the 'language groups'. See the next page to discover which group you belong to.

Answer key

When you see this icon, it signifies that the answers for this exercise can be found in the answer key on page 146.

Language groups

This book is designed to be used by anybody who speaks English as a second language. We have divided many of the languages of the world into eight groups, based on the similarities native speakers of these languages usually demonstrate in the way they pronounce the sounds of English. Consequently, you may find that you are in a group where your native language is very different from others in that group. *Trust us!* It's not about your native language – it's about how that language affects your English.

1	Cantonese, Japanese, Korean, Indonesian, Malay, Mandarin, Thai, Vietnamese
2	French, Italian, Spanish, Tagalog
3	Bengali, Urdu, all languages of India
4	Czech, Estonian, Latvian, Lithuanian, Polish, Russian, Slovak, Slovene, Tajik, Ukrainian
5	Arabic, Farsi, Hebrew, Pashto
6	Afrikaans, Danish, Dutch, Finnish, German, Icelandic, Norwegian, Swedish
7	Languages of sub-Saharan Africa
8	Bulgarian, Croatian, Greek, Hungarian, Moldovan, Portuguese, Romanian, Serbian, Turkish, Uzbek

 **1 2 3 4 5 6 7 8** When you see this icon, check to see if your group number is listed. If it is, you should pay particular attention to that point.

Of course, these groups aren't absolute – our accents are individual to us, contain huge variation and change all the time. But you can use the language groups as a quick guide to the sounds that are likely to be the most important for you to work on. We still recommend reading all of the instructions, and practising everything in this book.

My first language isn't there!

If you speak a language not listed here and you're not sure which group you belong in, think about which of the languages listed are most similar to your first language. If your first language is similar, you are likely to have similar habits when speaking English.

Section A

Getting started

Accent softening

Let's just get this out there: WE LOVE ACCENTS!

We are accent coaches, so we spend our days listening to, working with, and enjoying accents of all varieties. We certainly aren't interested in forcing everyone to speak one way, so that we all sound the same – how boring would that be? What we *are* interested in is helping people to communicate as clearly and freely as possible.

Why do I have an accent?

Everyone in the world has an accent when they speak. One accent is no better than any other. However, people who speak English as a second language regularly ask us for help with English pronunciation in order to stop people misunderstanding the things that they say. It's frustrating to be asked to repeat yourself, or to feel that people are listening to how you are speaking, rather than what you are saying. This book will help you to understand how small changes to your pronunciation can make a big difference to how well you are understood.

Why soften my accent?

There are a number of reasons why you may want to soften your accent. They may not all apply to you and you may have reasons of your own, but these are some of the most common:

- People make judgements about us when we speak, both professional and personal judgements. We may not like it, but they do.

- A strong accent may often be perceived as a low language level, which is frustrating for the speaker and can lead to missed opportunities in work and everyday life.

- A strong accent, even with perfect grammar and vocabulary, can prevent understanding and make you feel less confident about communicating.

In reality, pronunciation is a separate skill and not a reflection of how fluent you are. However, the way that we speak also affects the way that we hear, so not understanding the rules of pronunciation can mean that some information is processed incorrectly, and can lead to misunderstandings and more missed opportunities.

How will it feel?

Working on your accent will feel very different from working on your grammar or vocabulary.

When you change how you speak, you change a part of your identity. Our voices and accents are highly personal reflections of who we are. When we speak, we instantly share information with the world about where we have come from and how we feel about ourselves. People respond to that information, and make judgements, even if they don't realize they are doing so. When you change the way you speak, people will respond to you differently, and you will also feel different about yourself.

People sometimes say they feel fake when they first start learning a new accent. This is unavoidable, so we recommend treating it as part of the fun! Give yourself permission to feel different at first, like putting on a disguise. You will gradually get more and more used to talking in this way.

And of course, you don't have to talk with this new accent all the time. You're not getting rid of the way you currently speak in your second language, but rather, learning another, different pronunciation system that you can use as and when you choose to. You'll also still be able to speak your native language with your original accent. Those pronunciations were learnt in childhood, and are very strongly established.

The need for mirror practice

When we decide to speak, we don't usually decide how we are going to move our mouths to make words. When we decide to say 'hello', we don't think about the individual sounds that make up that word: we don't decide how to make the *h*, then the *e*, then the *ll*, then the *o* sounds – that would take forever! Speaking is an automatic process – our tongue and lips just go where they are used to going. But when you are working on your accent, you do need to start breaking words up into sounds, and consciously thinking about how your mouth, tongue and lips are moving.

Because the movement of the *mobile articulators* (see page 8) is subconscious during daily speech, it can be hard to control them when you first start working on your accent. Sometimes it will feel like you're doing something that in reality you aren't doing at all. For example, it may feel like you are leaving your lips neutral, when you are actually rounding them. For this reason, we recommend using a mirror when you are practising, at least at first.

Let's try an experiment. Look at the illustration below showing the lip-rounding for the *oo* in the word 'goose'.

Say 'goose', copying the lip position in the photo above. What do your lips feel like they are doing? Do they feel rounded or neutral?

Now, look in the mirror and make the same sound again. What are your lips *really* doing? Were they more like one of these ?

Now, still looking in the mirror, make the same shape as the target picture. This is the correct position for this sound. If it feels unnatural, you are already learning a new sound!

It is important that you always practise with a mirror, at least until you are confident that you are very familiar with the movement of the mobile articulators and you can move them accurately for each sound.

When you first start using this book, make sure you always have a mirror to hand as you are watching the video clips and that you are continuously comparing yourself to the speakers. If you don't do this you may be reinforcing a mistake or, worse still, learning a whole new error. It is important to do this even for sounds that feel very obvious.

What accent will I learn?

The British English accent you will be learning in this book is called Received Pronunciation, or RP for short. Geographically, RP is most commonly associated with the south of England, and is one of the main accents spoken in and around London, although certainly not the only one. Queen Elizabeth II speaks a very traditional form of RP, while many British TV and radio presenters speak one which is more typical of modern-day users.

RP has changed a lot over the years, and in this book we will use a modern version of the accent so that you don't end up speaking like a character from a period drama. Not all British people sound like they should be living in the 1800s and sipping tea with Jane Austen, so you should not speak that way either!

So what will this accent say about me?

We think it's important that you understand what the accent in this book will tell people about you and there are some broad generalizations that could be made about someone who is a native speaker of RP.

Among native speakers, RP is geographically associated with the south-east of England, and socially with the middle class, or people in professional positions.

Historically speaking, the modern RP that we are using in this book will be more typical of people born after 1960, and you will find occasional notes in the text about sounds that are currently evolving.

RP is the usual pronunciation standard in EFL teaching in the UK.

The anatomy of speech

As we speak, we repeat certain sounds over and over again in different patterns that we call words. The muscles of our mouths develop patterns and habits through these repetitions. Talking is like body-building for the mouth – and it's a very regular workout!

The habits we build are specific to our native language and accent. If you speak English, using the muscle habits from your native language, you will have an obvious international accent. So, if you want to learn RP, you need to retrain the muscles in your mouth to behave in a different and unfamiliar way.

Talking may not seem like an athletic activity, but the process of learning a new accent sound system is no different to learning gymnastics. You need to retrain your muscles to handle the new moves!

And just like gymnastics, the more regularly you practise, the better and faster you will see results.

In order to learn these new muscular patterns, you need to understand how your voice works and you'll also need to learn some technical terms to explain how your voice works.

How your voice works

This is what happens when we speak:

1 Inhalation: We breathe in – air comes into the lungs. Air is the fuel of speech.
2 Exhalation: We start to breathe out.
3 Voicing: As the air moves through the larynx, the vocal folds vibrate and turn it into sound.
4 Resonance: The sound gets amplified, as it vibrates in the body.
5 Articulation: The mouth moves to create individual speech sounds which combine to make words.

The larynx

The larynx is another name for the voice box. It is also sometimes called the Adam's Apple. It's the bit that sticks out in the front of your neck and is more obvious in men than women. Inside the larynx is a set of very tiny muscles called the vocal folds. As we exhale, air passes up from our lungs, through the larynx, making the vocal folds vibrate. When the vocal folds vibrate, they turn this air into voiced sound.

DVD

Try this exercise:

- Put your hand on your larynx (front of your neck) and say the sound 'aaaah'. Even if you say it quietly, you will feel vibration under your hand. That is the vocal folds vibrating.
- Keep your hand in the same place and this time whisper the sound 'aaaaah'. Now you won't feel any vibration, because the air is passing straight through the vocal folds.
- Sounds which make the larynx vibrate are called *voiced* and those which don't are called *voiceless*.

Some consonant sounds exist in voiced and voiceless pairs. This means you do exactly the same thing with your mouth for both sounds, but just add or remove voicing in the larynx.

- Let's practise this with the consonant pair /s/ and /z/.
- Put your hand on your larynx: say the sound /z/ as in 'zoo'. You will feel vibration under your hand.
- Keep your hand on your larynx: now whisper the sound /z/. You will not feel any vibration under your hand.
- A whispered /z/ is a /s/ sound! /z/ is voiced and /s/ is unvoiced, but in every other way they are identical.

The articulators

The articulators are the parts of the mouth that are responsible for turning sound into speech. We have two types– **fixed articulators** and **mobile articulators**.

The **fixed articulators** are made of bone. They form part of the framework of the mouth so we cannot move them or train them to do something different. These are: the *teeth*, the *alveolar ridge* and the *hard palate*.

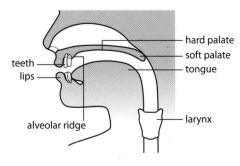

- Look at the illustration above, and note where the fixed articulators are. While you will know where your teeth are, you may not have heard of the other two before, but you will almost certainly have used them in speech.

- To find your alveolar ridge, run your tongue tip backwards from the back of your top front teeth. After you pass the top of the teeth you will find a little bump – this is the alveolar ridge.

- Just after the bump you will feel the roof of the mouth swoop into a large curve, which feels hard – this is the hard palate.

These three essential articulators never move, so instead we move the other, mobile articulators to touch them.

The **mobile articulators** are muscles, so they can move. These are the *tongue*, the *lips* and the *soft palate*. It is these articulators that we need to retrain to learn a different accent. It is essential that you understand these articulators so that you can form new habits.

The tongue

The tongue is the most important articulator. For the RP accent, there are two general rules:

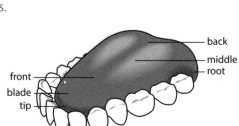

- The back of the tongue has to be very relaxed and dropped, to make a lot of space in the back of the mouth.

- The tip of the tongue has to be flexible and dynamic. This is the main tool in creating many of the crisp consonants found in English.

DVD

Try this exercise to get your tongue ready for the sounds and movements of RP:

- Put out your tongue, and alternate between pointing and relaxing it.

- Curl the tip of your tongue upwards, so that it touches your lips, then teeth, then alveolar ridge. Repeat this several times.

- Put the tip of your tongue on the back of your lower teeth, then yawn, without letting the tip move. Notice the stretch that you feel in the back of your tongue.

The lips

The lips can dramatically change a sound because of the huge number of ways they can be shaped and manipulated. Here are some general guidelines for producing a good RP accent:

- The lips have to be very flexible.

- The corners of the lips should be relaxed, to allow more vertical movement than horizontal.

- Rounded lip shapes are very common in this accent.

DVD Try this exercise to get your lips ready for the sounds and movements of RP:

- Relax your lips and blow through them, making them flap. This will make a sound a bit like a horse.

- Screw your face up as small as you possibly can, and then stretch your face out. Repeat this several times.

The soft palate

The soft palate is the flap that separates the nose from the mouth. You can't see it (unless you open your mouth really wide and look in a mirror!) and you probably don't even know it's doing anything when you speak, but it is extremely important. It can open and close to control whether air passes through your nose or your mouth.

To feel this working, start to exhale through your mouth, and then half way through, change and finish exhaling through your nose. You should feel something move – this is your soft palate.

To produce a good RP accent, the soft palate has to be very responsive. It is completely lifted on all vowels and most consonants meaning the sound comes out through your mouth – these are *oral* sounds, but it is fully lowered for /m/, /n/ and /ŋ/ sounds meaning the sound comes out through your nose – these are *nasal* sounds.

DVD Try this exercise to get your soft palate ready for the sounds and movements of RP:

- Pinch and release your nose while saying the vowel sound 'aaaaa'. The sound should not change at all. If you hear some change in the sound, try yawning and notice the difference. This happens because when we yawn, the soft palate automatically lifts.

- Now try swapping between a completely nasal sound like /m/ and a vowel. Check that the vowel you produce is completely oral by pinching your nose.

The jaw

The jaw is the *almost*-articulator. We call it this because it is the only articulator that we want to become less active in order to speak English more clearly. A free and relaxed jaw allows the rest of the articulators to move more freely and makes speech easier. Tension in the jaw will always prevent clear speech in English. Here are some guidelines to producing a good RP accent:

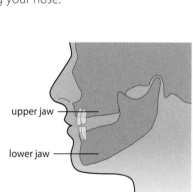

- The jaw should be very relaxed in order to produce the open vowel sounds

- Many accents don't open the jaw wide enough to create the sounds for RP English. For this reason you should work at loosening the jaw so you are able to produce the more open vowel sounds.

DVD Try this exercise to get your jaw ready for the sounds and movements of RP:

- Put your hands on the side of your face, clench your teeth, and then relax.

- Notice the place where you felt the muscle tensing.

- Now start to massage that area, whilst thinking of space being created between your molar teeth.

Why use the IPA?

English is a famously difficult language to pronounce. This is because, unlike many other languages, it is not phonetic. This means you do not say all the sounds that you see written on the page and sometimes you add some that aren't there at all. Sometimes the same spellings can produce different sounds in different words, and often the same sound is produced by a variety of spellings.

Look at these two pictures:

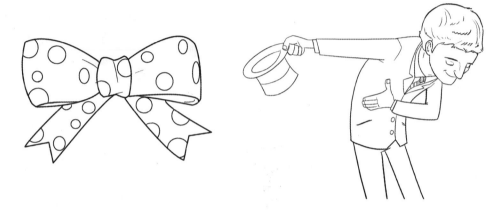

The same title could be given to both of these pictures: 'A bow'. In writing, there is no way of telling the difference between the two, but the two words sound quite different. For this reason, the International Phonetic Alphabet (or IPA) is extremely useful when working on your accent.

Speaking, not spelling

The IPA is a way of transcribing the sounds that you hear, rather than relying on the way words are written. In the IPA, the picture on the left above is represented as /bəʊ/, but the picture on the right is /bæʊ/.

In order to use the IPA, you will need to stop thinking about spelling. For example, how many vowels are there in English? If we think in terms of spelling, the answer is five: *a, e, i, o,* and *u.* But if we think in terms of the sound that we hear, there are many more. For example, look at the different sounds that can be made by the letter *a.*

- bat
- bath
- bake
- want
- walk
- bead
- bread
- learn

That's eight different vowel sounds, all from just from one vowel letter!

Use of the IPA in *Work on your Accent*

Section B of this book works through each of the different sounds of RP. You will see the phonetic symbols for each sound at the top of the page. You don't need to become an expert in phonetics to use this book, but an awareness of the IPA will help you to think in terms of sound, rather than spelling, which is the only way to improve your English pronunciation.

However, we know that sometimes the IPA symbols can look confusing. So throughout the book you will also use the phonetic symbol alongside a *keyword* to refer to each sound. These same words are used in the unit titles (e.g. /p/ as in PET, /b/ as in BET, and /ʊ/ as in FOOT made by the letters *oo*) . This means you don't need to memorize the IPA symbols, just recognize the sound in context.

Below, there is a quick reference table containing all of the sounds and keywords we use. Mark this page, and you can refer back to it any time you need to while using this book.

The sounds of RP

CONSONANTS		VOWELS	
/p/	as in **P**ET	/ə/	as in LETT**ER**, COMM**A**
/b/	as in **B**ET	/ɜː/	as in N**UR**SE
/t/	as in **T**O	/ɪ/	as in K**I**T
/d/	as in **D**O	/iː/	as in SH**EE**P
/k/	as in **C**OT	/e/	as in DR**E**SS
/g/	as in **G**OT	/æ/	as in C**A**P
/m/	as in **M**E	/ʌ/	as in C**U**P
/n/	as in **N**O	/ɑː/	as in B**A**TH
/ŋ/	as in SI**NG**	/ʊ/	as in F**OO**T
/s/	as in **S**OON	/uː/	as in G**OO**SE
/z/	as in **Z**OOM	/ɒ/	as in L**O**T
/f/	as in **F**AST	/ɔː/	as in TH**OU**GHT
/v/	as in **V**AST		
/tʃ/	as in **CH**OKE		
/dʒ/	as in **J**OKE	/əʊ/	as in G**OA**T
/θ/	as in **TH**IN	/æʊ/	as in M**OU**TH
/ð/	as in **TH**IS	/eɪ/	as in F**A**CE
/ʃ/	as in **SH**INE	/ʌɪ/	as in PR**I**CE
/ʒ/	as in TREA**S**URE	/ɔɪ/	as in CH**OI**CE
/l/	as in **L**OVE	/ɪə/	as in N**EAR**
/ɫ/	as in HI**LL**	/eə/	as in H**AIR**
/h/	as in **H**ELLO	/ʊə/	as in C**URE**
/j/	as in **Y**ES		
/w/	as in **W**EEK		
/ɹ/	as in **R**OCK		

The sounds of English

The consonant sounds

Consonants are sounds for which the airflow is obstructed as it leaves the mouth. This means that you have to make **strong movements** to produce each of these sounds. So to make a consonant sound, you need to know which of the **articulators** make the obstruction. (See page 8 for a reminder of what the fixed and mobile articulators are.) Sometimes two mobile articulators touch each other (like for the sound 'b' – **b**ee), and for other sounds one of the mobile articulators moves and touches one of the fixed articulators (like for the sound 'd' – **d**o).

The amount of obstruction varies but all of them require you to obstruct the airflow, unlike vowel sounds. This means that some consonant sounds can be extended for a long time, while others are short sharp sounds. Try making sounds like 'm' (**m**e), 'w' (**w**e), 's' (**s**o), 'f' (**f**ar), and notice how they can all be held on, while 'p' (**p**ea), 't' (**t**ea) and 'k' (**k**ey) are all short and can't be extended.

Different types of consonant sounds

We can divide the consonants of RP into six groups based on how they are made. Knowing which group the sounds fall into in English will help you to tell the difference between two sounds which might sound more similar in your first language than they should in English.

- **Explosive sounds (known as 'plosives')**

  These sounds start with a complete blockage which is then suddenly released. These sounds are:

/p/ (**p**et)	/t/ (**t**o)	/k/ (**c**ot)
/b/ (**b**et)	/d/ (**d**o)	/g/ (**g**ot)

- **Friction sounds (known as 'fricatives')**

  For these sounds there is less of an obstruction so a stream of air is able to escape through a small space. These sounds are:

/f/ (**f**ish)	/ʒ/ (trea**s**ure)	/s/ (**s**oon)
/v/ (**v**et)	/θ/ (**th**in)	/z/ (**z**oom)
/ʃ/ (**sh**ine)	/ð/ (**th**en)	/h/ (**h**ello)

- **Combination sounds (known as 'affricates')**

  These are consonants that start as an explosive sound then become a friction sound. The blockage is complete at the start but is then released slowly. These sounds are:

/tʃ/ (**ch**oke)	/dʒ/ (**j**oke)

- **Sounds made through the nose (known as 'nasals')**

  These are the consonants where the sound comes entirely out of the nose with no breath leaving through the mouth. These sounds are:

/n/ (**n**o)	/m/ (**m**e)	/ŋ/ (si**ng**)

- **Side sounds (known as 'laterals')**

  These are sounds where the sound is released round the sides of the tongue.

  /l/ (**l**ove)   /ɫ/ (hi**ll**)

- **Open sounds (known as 'approximants')**

  These sounds don't have an obvious contact point, but the articulators almost create a blockage by getting very close to each other but not quite touching. This is the least obstruction it's possible to make while still being a consonant sound. These sounds are:

  /ɹ/ (**r**ed)   /j/ (**y**es)   /w/ (**w**eek)

Voiced and voiceless sounds

Some consonant sounds are **voiced** (e.g. /b/ and /z/), and some are **voiceless** (e.g. /p/ and /s/). For voiced consonants the vocal folds (in your larynx) vibrate, and for voiceless sounds there is no vibration.

Some consonant sounds exist in 'voiced and voiceless pairs' (e.g. /t/ and /d/ are a pair). This means you do exactly the same thing with your mouth for both sounds, but just add or remove voicing in the larynx. (For more explanation of this, turn back to page 7.) We cover the identical voiced/voiceless pairs of sounds in the same units. So a sound like /n/ (**n**o), which has no voiceless partner, has a unit to itself. But a pair of sounds like /t/ and /d/ (**t**o/**d**o), which are voiced/voiceless partners, are both covered in the same unit.

Making the sound

To make each consonant sound, you need to know:

- Where in the mouth the airflow is obstructed.
- How much of an obstruction is made to the airflow.
- Whether the sound is voiced or voiceless.

If you get these three things right, you will produce the right sound. So let's get started!

PET & BET

/p/ (**p**et), /b/ (**b**et)

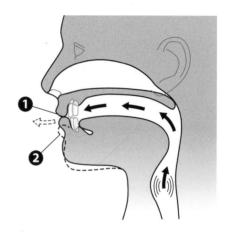

Make the sounds

DVD

1 Lightly squeeze your lips together, all the way along.

2 Start to breathe out, and let a little air build up behind your lips.

3 Don't let any air out through your nose!

4 Let your lips spring apart quickly, and continue breathing out.

5 The sound you produce can be voiced /b/ or voiceless /p/ (see page 15).

When do I use this sound?

2

Voiced/voiceless	Spelling	Examples	Frequency
voiceless	*p*	pen, cup, open	often
voiceless	*pp*	apple, appear	often
voiced	*b*	be, able, stumble, cab	often
voiced	*bb*	stubble	often

! There is a silent *b* in *mb* spellings like 'comb', 'womb', 'dumb'.

Now try it!

Say each of these words and sentences aloud. Then compare your pronunciation with the model on tracks 3–5.

3–5

A 1   pen   price   carpet   open   appear   cup   stop

      2   birthday   boss   able   above   tub   tube

B 1   Please press play, pause and stop on the tape.

      2   Both boys bought big bunches of bananas.

      3   The perfect place to spend your birthday is on the beach with your best pals.

C 1   I'd like a proper cup of coffee from a proper copper coffee pot.

      2   A big black bug bit a big brown bear, and the big brown bear bled badly.

Am I doing something wrong?

 **All groups**

✗   Not adding an extra puff of air for a /**p**/ sound.

✓   Make sure to allow a small extra puff of air as your lips spring apart if:

   • /**p**/ is the first sound in a word ('pen') or it is in the stressed syllable ('appear'), and

   • it is followed by a vowel

You don't need this puff of air if the /**p**/ is followed by a consonant ('price'), is unstressed ('carpet'), or is at the end of a word ('cup').

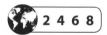 **2 4 6 8**

✗   Making the same sound in the words 'pet' and 'bet'.

✓   First, revise the exercises for how to make voiced and voiceless sounds (page 7).

Then, revise the *When do I use this sound?* table for /**p**/ and /**b**/.

Keep a hand on your larynx while you practise, and check whether you are adding vibration or not.

 2 3

✗   Bringing your lips very close to each other, but not totally blocking the breath.

✓   Make sure that you are closing your lips all the way along, and then releasing them quickly.

17

TO & DO
/t/ (**t**o), /d/ (**d**o)

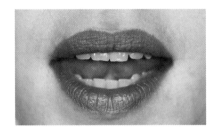
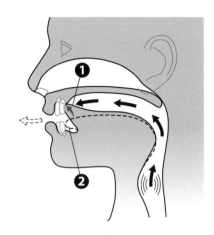

Make the sounds

DVD

1 Press the tip of your tongue onto the alveolar ridge.

2 Let the sides of your tongue touch the top molars.

3 Start to breathe out, and let a little air build up behind your tongue.

4 Don't let any air out through your nose!

5 Drop your tongue tip quickly, and continue breathing out.

6 The sound you produce can be voiced /d/ or voiceless /t/ (see page 15).

When do I use this sound?

6

Voiced/voiceless	Spelling	Examples	Frequency
voiceless	*t*	top, atom, sat	often
voiceless	*tt*	butter	often
voiceless	*th*	Thomas, Thailand, thyme	rarely, just in names/places
voiced	*d*	do, meadow, brand	often
voiced	*dd*	ladder	often

! There is a silent *t* if *st* is in the middle of the word like 'fasten', 'listen', 'whistle', 'glisten', 'castle', 'hustle'.

/t/ and /d/ sounds are sometimes not released on the ends of words. You will find an explanation of this in the section on *Connecting your speech* (page 91).

Now try it!

Say each of these words and sentences aloud. Then compare your pronunciation with the model on tracks 7–9.

7–9

A **1** time   train   artist   attain   bottom   heart   late

2 dog   drive   rider   India   read   hard   ready

B	**1**	Tell Tom to take the train into town.
	2	Daisy couldn't decide which day to drive down to Dover.
C	**1**	A tiny tiger tied her tie tighter, to tidy her tatty tail.
	2	Dotty tried to do too much so Dotty ended up drained.

Am I doing something wrong?

   ✗   Putting your tongue tip somewhere other than your alveolar ridge.

   ✓   Be sure that your tongue tip is on the alveolar ridge behind your teeth. Not touching your teeth, and not curling too far backwards behind the alveolar ridge.

   ✗   Not adding an extra puff of air for a /t/ sound.

   ✓   Make sure to allow a small extra puff of air as your lips spring apart if /t/ is the first sound in a word ('time') or is the stressed syllable ('attain'), and it is followed by a vowel.

       You don't need this puff of air if the /t/ is followed by a consonant ('train'), is unstressed ('bottom'), or is at the end of a word ('heart').

All groups

   ✗   Making 'heart' and 'hard' sound the same.

   ✓   First, revise the exercises for how to make voiced and voiceless sounds (page 7).

       Then, revise the *When do I use this sound?* tables above for /t/ and /d/.

       Keep a hand on your larynx while you practise, and check whether you are adding vibration or not.

2 3 5 6 8

   ✗   Not blocking the air completely, and adding voicing so that /t/ sounds between vowels become similar to a /d/.

   ✓   Block the air completely, and then release it quickly, rather than flicking the tongue tip onto the alveolar ridge. Make sure that the /t/ sound is unvoiced.

1 2 8

   ✗   Blocking the airflow in your throat, rather than with the tongue tip. This is called a glottal stop.

   ✓   Keep breathing out through the sound, rather than stopping the air in your larynx. Check that you hear the sound of your tongue releasing the air.

COT & **G**OT

/k/ (**c**ot), /g/ (**g**ot)

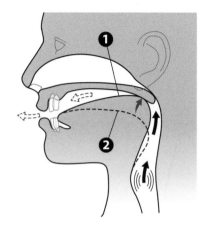

Make the sounds

DVD

1. Raise the back of your tongue to touch the back of the roof of your mouth.
2. Start to breathe out, and let a little air build up behind your tongue.
3. Don't let any air out through your nose!
4. Drop the back of your tongue down quickly, letting the air out of your mouth.
5. The sound you produce can be voiced /g/ or voiceless /k/ (see page 15).

When do I use this sound?

10

Voiced/voiceless	Spelling	Examples	Frequency
voiceless	c, cc, k, ck	cat, soccer, key, back	often
voiceless	ch	chord, ache	sometimes
voiceless (+/w/)	qu	quit, aqua	often
voiceless (+/s/)	x (irregular)	exit, six	often
voiced	g, gg	get, again, bigger	often
voiced	gh, gu	ghost, guess	sometimes
voiced	x (irregular)	examine, exotic	sometimes

> ! There is a silent *k* in *kn* spellings at the start of words like 'know', 'knee', 'knife'.
>
> There can be a silent *g* in *gn* spellings like 'gnome' and 'sign'.
>
> The *g* in *gh* spellings is not usually pronounced as a /g/. Sometimes it is silent ('through'), and other times *gh* is pronounced /f/ ('enough').

Now try it!

Say each of these words and sentences aloud. Then compare your pronunciation with the model on tracks 11–13.

11–13

A **1** <u>c</u>at <u>cl</u>ean e<u>ch</u>o re<u>c</u>ord ba<u>ck</u> as<u>k</u> si<u>x</u>

    2 <u>g</u>et <u>g</u>reen ar<u>g</u>ue a<u>g</u>ain ba<u>g</u> do<u>g</u> di<u>gg</u>er

B **1** Excuse me, could you bake me a cream cake?

    2 The girl got good grades in her exams.

C **1** Six quick cricket critics.

    2 A gaggle of grey geese are in the green grass grazing.

Am I doing something wrong?

 **All groups**

✗ Not adding an extra puff of air for a /k/ sound.

✓ Make sure to allow a small extra puff of air as your lips spring apart if:

    ● /k/ is the first sound in a word ('cat') or is the stressed syllable ('record' *verb*),

and

    ● it is followed by a vowel.

You don't need this puff of air if the /k/ is followed by a consonant ('clean'), is unstressed ('record' *noun*), or is at the end of a word ('back').

 **All groups**

✗ Using the same sound in 'back' and 'bag'.

✓ First, revise the exercises for how to make voiced and voiceless sounds (page 7).

Then, revise the *When do I use this sound?* table above for /k/ and /g/.

Keep a hand on your larynx while you practise, so that you can check whether you are adding vibration or not.

 4 8

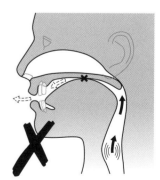

✗ Using the middle of your tongue, rather than the back. If you feel your tongue pressing against the highest part of the roof of your mouth – this is wrong.

✓ The back of your tongue should touch your soft palate, which is further back in your mouth.

> The letter *c* can often be pronounced with a /s/ sound. For more rules on this, turn to the /s/ page (page 28).

4

ME /m/

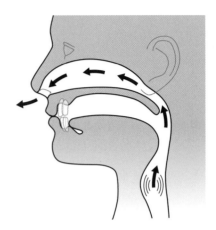

Make the sound

DVD

1 Lightly squeeze your lips together, all the way along.

2 Breathe out through your nose.

3 This sound is always voiced.

When do I use this sound?

14

Spelling	Examples	Frequency
m	me, amaze, film	often
mm	swimmer	often
mb	comb, womb, dumb	rarely
mn	autumn, condemn	rarely

Now try it!

Say each of these words and sentences aloud. Then compare your pronunciation with the model on tracks 15–17.

15–17

A <u>m</u>e mo<u>st</u> ar<u>m</u>y i<u>m</u>age fil<u>m</u> co<u>m</u>e

B **1** My mum will be missing me, and waiting for me to come home tomorrow.

2 I was dreaming about the shimmering moon on Monday.

3 It's a shame that the man is so mean to his team.

C **1** My mate Mike makes me mad.

2 Many an anemone sees an enemy anemone.

Am I doing something wrong?

✗   Not fully touching your lips together when you make this sound.

✓   Use a mirror to check that your lips are completely closed. You should be able to feel the lips gently pressing against each other.

Assimilation in nasal sounds

Sometimes when we are speaking quickly, one sound changes to become more like the sound next to it. This does make speech easier and faster, and as RP evolves, more and more speakers use these assimilations in their speech.

This very often happens with nasal sounds like /m/, /n/, and /ŋ/. Look at these examples:

Green Park   can sound like   *GreemPark*

The /n/ sound at the end of 'green' has become more similar to the /p/ of 'park', and is being made on the lips like a /m/.

some time   can sound like   *suntime*

The /m/ sound at the end of 'some' has become more similar to the /t/ sound of 'time', and is being made with the tongue tip on the alveolar ridge like a /n/.

run clumsily   can sound like   *rungclumsily*

The /n/ sound at the end of 'run' has become more similar to the /k/ sound of 'clumsily', and is being made with the tongue on the soft palate like a /ŋ/.

young lady   can sound like   *younlady*

The /ŋ/ sound of 'young' has become more similar to the /l/ sound of 'lady' and is being made with the tongue on the alveolar ridge like a /n/.

Now try it!

Try saying the following sentences first without and then with assimilation. Remember, assimilation only happens when you are speaking quickly.

1   Can both of them try to find jobs when college is over?

2   It's a long time since that man has driven cars in races.

3   I don't mean to seem depressed, but there are not many fun games being played lately.

4   I can put some time aside to ring Dad later on Monday.

NO /n/

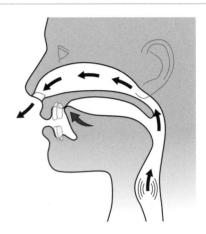

Make the sound

DVD

1 Put the tip of your tongue on the alveolar ridge.
2 Let the sides of your tongue rest on the top molars.
3 Breathe out through your nose.
4 This sound is always voiced.

When do I use this sound?

18

Spelling	Examples	Frequency
n	no, any, run	often
nn	winner, annoy	often
gn	gnaw, sign	sometimes
kn	know, knee, knife	sometimes

! There is a silent *n* in *mn* spellings like 'column', 'autumn', 'condemn'.

Now try it!

Say each of these words and sentences aloud. Then compare your pronunciation with the model on tracks 19–21.

A   <u>n</u>o   <u>n</u>ear   a<u>n</u>y   se<u>n</u>d   ru<u>n</u>   <u>n</u>o<u>n</u>e   su<u>n</u>

B   **1**   There are not nearly enough chances to change.

   2   The day can only begin when someone turns on the news.

   3   The company is open, and it's business as normal on Monday.

C   **1**   Nine noisy nurses knot nine nice knots.

   2   Nobody knew Nina when Nina was a nobody.

Am I doing something wrong?

 1 2 3 4 5 7 8

✗   Putting the tongue tip in the wrong place.

✓   Be sure that your tongue tip is on the alveolar ridge behind your teeth. Check that your tongue tip isn't touching your teeth, and that it isn't curling too far backwards behind the alveolar ridge.

 1 2

✗   Raising the back of your tongue up to touch your soft palate and making the same sound in the words 'sun' and 'sung'.

✓   Relax the back of your tongue so that it is low in your mouth, like a yawn. Review the rules of when to use /n/ and when to use /ŋ/ (page 26).

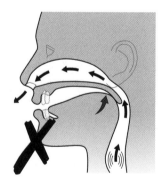

 1 2

✗   Not raising the tongue tip to touch the alveolar ridge, and just making the resulting vowel sound through the nose instead. This nasal vowel sound does not exist in RP.

✓   Be sure that you can feel your tongue tip making contact with the alveolar ridge.

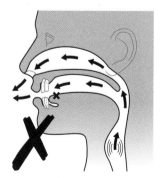

SING /ŋ/

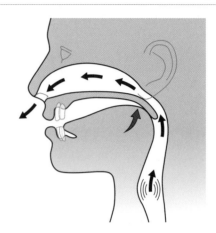

Make the sound

DVD

1 Raise the back of your tongue to touch the soft palate, as if you're going to make a /g/ sound, as in 'go'.

2 Check that your tongue tip is relaxed in the bottom of your mouth.

3 Breathe out through your nose.

4 This sound is always voiced.

When do I use this sound?

22

Spelling	Examples	Frequency
ng	song, singer, walking	often
nk or *nc* spellings /ŋk/	think, banker, uncle	often
ng in the middle of a word, not followed by a suffix /ŋg/	hunger, language, engage, finger	often
ng in comparative or superlative words /ŋg/	stronger, longest	often

Now try it!

Say each of these words and sentences aloud. Then compare your pronunciation with the model on tracks 23–25.

23–25

A lo<u>ng</u> si<u>ng</u>er waiti<u>ng</u> fi<u>ng</u>er thi<u>n</u>k ba<u>n</u>ker

B   **1**   I think it's wrong to be sitting and waiting for something exciting.

   2   The phone is ringing, but it's the bank calling.

   3   Walking all the way to the meeting will take a long time.

C   **1**   Sitting and thinking of swimming and singing.

Am I doing something wrong?

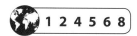

✗   Pronouncing a /g/ sound after the /ŋ/ in words like 'bang' and 'wrong'. The *g* spelling is part of this /ŋ/ sound, rather than a separate sound to be added to the end of the word.

✓   Stop breathing out before you drop the back of your tongue down.

   This sound is a sustainable sound, and has no defining end point. Practise by holding onto the sound for longer than is normal, until you get used to ending it in this way.

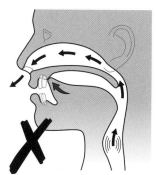

✗   Using the same sound in the words 'sun' and 'sung'.

✓   Check that the front of your tongue is relaxed, and not rising up to touch the alveolar ridge.

✗   Not actually raising the tongue back to make the closure and so sending the vowel sound through the nose. This will sound like a nasal vowel, rather than a consonant /ŋ/.

✓   Be sure that you can feel the back of your tongue touching your soft palate.

Sometimes, the *g* in an *ng* spelling is pronounced as a separate sound, making the sounds /ŋg/. Look at the table below:

1 /ŋg/	2 /ŋ/	3 /ŋg/
hunger, finger, linger, language, anger, engage, dangle	longing, longed, hangman, hanger	longer, longest, stronger, strongest

1 If *ng* spelling is in the middle of a word (other than a word with a suffix, like *-ed*, *-ing*, *-er*) then the /ŋg/ pronunciation is used.

2 When a suffix, or additional word, is added to the root word, /ŋ/ is the usual pronunciation.

3 However, if you are using the comparative or superlative suffixes, *-est* and *-er*, the /ŋg/ pronunciation is used again.

!   You should always pronounce the /k/ sound in words with *nk* combinations, e.g. 'think', 'thank you'.

SOON & ZOOM /s/ (**s**oon), /z/ (**z**oom)

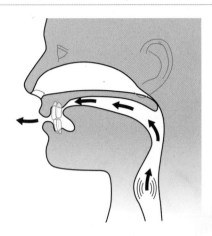

Make the sounds

DVD

1 People make this sound in different ways, sometimes with the tongue tip up, sometimes with the tongue tip down. It doesn't really matter which you do.

2 The important thing is to raise the blade of your tongue up until it is very close to your alveolar ridge, without actually touching it, and then breathe out.

3 As the air is pushed between your tongue and your alveolar ridge, you make a hissing sound.

5 The sound you produce can be voiced /z/ or voiceless /s/ (see page 15).

When do I use this sound?

26

Voiced/voiceless	Spelling	Examples	Frequency
voiceless	s	sad, inside, this	often
voiceless	ss	glass, missing	often
voiceless	c	cycle, nice, acid	often
voiceless	sc	scene, descend	sometimes
voiceless (+/k/)	x	exercise, sixty	sometimes
voiced	z	zoo, amazing	often
voiced	s (after a voiced sound)	roads, days, fools	often
voiced	zz	fizzy	sometimes
voiced	ss	scissors	sometimes
voiced (+ /g/)	x	example	sometimes
voiced	-ize/-ise verb endings	organise, realize	sometimes

> **!** Sometimes *s* is not pronounced as a /s/, like in 'sugar' and 'issue'. In these case it becomes a /ʃ/ (see Unit 11).
>
> Pronunciation of *s* and *z* can depend on the grammar. In the noun 'use' and the adjective 'close' the *s* is pronounced /s/. But in the verbs 'use' and 'close' the same spellings are pronounced /z/.

Now try it!

Say each of these words and sentences aloud. Then compare your pronunciation with the model on tracks 27–29.

A **1** s͟ee   s͟top   bos͟s͟   fac͟e   s͟chool   fix͟   peac͟e

   2 z͟ip   laz͟y   goes͟   us͟e   ris͟e   ex͟am   peas͟

B **1** We must stop skipping school so we learn something.

   2 He's crazily lazy: he always refuses to use the gym.

   3 The office is closed on Sundays and most Tuesdays.

C **1** Six saints sat in silence in the sunshine.

   2 Zebras zig and zebras zag – crazy zig-zagging zebras!

Am I doing something wrong?

> **✗** Using the same sound in the words 'peas' and 'peace'.
>
> **✓** First, review the exercises for how to make voiced and voiceless sounds (page 7).
>
> Then, revise the *When do I use this sound?* table for /s/ and /z/.
>
> Keep a hand on your larynx while you practise, and check whether you are adding vibration or not.

> **✗** Making the same sound in the words 'she' and 'see'.
>
> **✓** Practise sliding your tongue forward towards your top teeth so that the sound gets a bit sharper.
>
> Make sure your lips are completely relaxed.

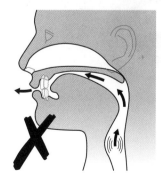

> /s/ can be a tricky sound for some people to produce even in their native language, and issues such as lisps are very common worldwide. This is not an accent issue. The best thing to do in this situation is to work with a trained speech and language therapist.

8

FAST & VAST

/f/ (**f**ast), /v/ (**v**ast)

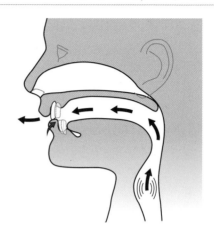

Make the sounds

DVD

1 Relax your tongue in your mouth – you don't need it for this sound.

2 Rest the very bottom edges of your top teeth on the inside of your bottom lip.

3 Keep the teeth and lip touching just enough to tickle your lip when you breathe out, but not so firmly that it completely blocks the airflow.

5 The sound you produce can be voiced /**v**/ or voiceless /**f**/ (see page 15).

When do I use this sound?

30

Voiced/voiceless	Spelling	Examples	Frequency
voiceless	*f*	feed, after, if	often
voiceless	*ff*	offer, cuff	often
voiceless	*gh*	enough, rough	sometimes
voiceless	*ph*	photo, telephone, graph	sometimes
voiced	*v*	vet, over, love	often

! The only exception to these rules is the word 'of', where you should use the /**v**/ sound.

Now try it!

Say each of these words and sentences aloud. Then compare your pronunciation with the model on tracks 31–33.

31–33

A **1**   <u>f</u>ish   <u>f</u>eel   a<u>f</u>ter   o<u>ff</u>ice   i<u>f</u>   lau<u>gh</u>   <u>ph</u>iloso<u>ph</u>y

2   <u>v</u>isit   <u>v</u>ote   a<u>v</u>oid   se<u>v</u>en   ca<u>v</u>e   lo<u>v</u>e   o<u>f</u>

B **1**   Travelling in Africa is very good fun.

2   My friend can't find his very valuable violin.

3   The staff in the government offices value their free time.

C **1**   Fred fries fresh fish on Fridays.

2   Vincent's village villa has very vibrant views.

Am I doing something wrong?

 1 2 4 6 8

✗   A common mistake is to bring the lip and teeth close together, but not close enough to touch. This produces a similar sound to the English /w/ in 'what'.

✓   Make sure that you can feel your top teeth gently touching the inside of your lower lip. The contact between lips and teeth is what makes the hissing sound. Your teeth should be inside your bottom lip, not outside. Check this in a mirror. The bottom tip of the top teeth should be hidden by the lower lip.

 1 2

✗   Making a short, sudden sound, like the /b/ as in 'bee', instead of a longer, breathy hiss.

✓   Practise holding a piece of paper between your lips and teeth, then make the /f/ and /v/ sounds without letting the paper drop. Keep practising the sounds with the paper in your mouth for five seconds. Now, remove the paper, and keep making the same sounds. Notice how the sound is continuous and feels a little ticklish – especially with the /v/.

9

CHOKE & JOKE /tʃ/ (**ch**oke), /dʒ/ (**j**oke)

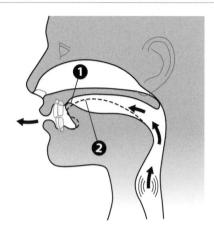

Make the sounds

DVD

1 This sound is made of two consonant sounds, so your tongue has to move in order to make it.

2 Practise making the /t/ as in 'tea', and the /ʃ/ as in 'shoe' (see pages 18 and 36).

3 Move quickly between the two sounds.

4 Get quicker and quicker until they begin to feel like one sound.

5 The sound you produce can be voiced /dʒ/ or voiceless /tʃ/ (see page 15).

When do I use this sound?

34

Voiced/voiceless	Spelling	Examples	Frequency
voiceless	*ch*	chair, teach	often
voiceless	*t*	nature	sometimes
voiceless	*tch*	catch	sometimes
voiced	*j*	job, banjo	often
voiced	*g*	gentle, age	sometimes
voiced	*dge*	edge	sometimes
voiced (+/n/)	*nge*	danger, angel, sponge	sometimes

Now try it!

Say each of these words and sentences aloud. Then compare your pronunciation with the model on tracks 35–37.

35–37

A **1** chin   chip   lecture   virtue   rich   batch

    2 judge   jail   giraffe·   major   damage   edge

B 1 There is too much cheap cheese in the kitchen.

2 The German judge made the arrangements on the edge of his seat.

3 I need a change, or perhaps I just need to imagine a new challenge for the future.

C 1 Cheap cheese tastes like chalk.

2 Jolly jugglers juggling jugs of orange juice.

Am I doing something wrong?

 1 2 6

✗ Making the same sound in the words 'ship' and 'chip'. You are missing out the first part of the sound (the /t/ or /d/), where your tongue touches the alveolar ridge.

✓ Focus on making the /t/ or /d/ sound, and then quickly sliding your tongue back into the /ʃ/ position. Try this practice exercise:

1	Say:	ship	ship	ship
2	Add a /t/ sound:	/t/ ship	/t/ ship	/t/ ship
3	Make the pause smaller:	/t/⌒ship	/t/⌒ship	/t/⌒ship
4	Until it feels like one sound:	chip	chip	chip

 1 6 8

✗ Making the same sound in the words 'gin' and 'chin'.

✓ First, revise the exercises for how to make voiced and voiceless sounds (page 7).

Then, revise the *When do I use this sound?* tables for /tʃ/ and /dʒ/.

Keep a hand on your larynx while you practise, and check whether you are adding vibration or not.

 4 8

✗ Making the same sound in the words 'bats' and 'batch'.

✓ Slide your tongue backwards a little as you drop it. Don't let it fall straight down. Try alternating between these sequences of sound pairs:

/t/⌒/s/ (as in SOON) /t/⌒/ʃ/ (as in SHINE)

/d/⌒/z/ (as in ZOOM) /t/⌒/ʒ/ (as in TREASURE)

Notice the different movements you feel in these two sets of sounds.

The movement in the right hand set of words is the correct way to form these sounds.

Now practise moving between the two parts of the sound more and more quickly, until they begin to sound and feel like one sound.

10

THIN & THIS /θ/ (**th**in), /ð/ (**th**is)

 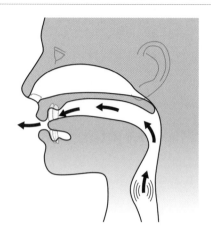

Make the sounds

DVD

1 Open your mouth a little so that there is some space between your top and bottom teeth.

2 Put the tip of your tongue lightly between the top and bottom teeth, keeping it relaxed.

3 Breathe out through your mouth.

4 Don't let any air out through your nose.

5 The sound you produce can be voiced /ð/ or voiceless /θ/ (see page 15).

When do I use this sound?

38

Voiced/voiceless	Spelling	Examples	Frequency
voiceless	*th*	think, three	often
voiceless	voiced consonant + *th*	month, seventh, width	often
voiced	*ther/the*	brother, other, breathe	often
voiced	*th*	those, these	often

! The spelling *th* is pronounced as a /t/ in some names and places, like Thomas, Thames and Thailand.

Now try it!

Say each of these words and sentences aloud. Then compare your pronunciation with the model on tracks 39–41.

39–41

A 1 think three ethical both earth path

2 they the weather other soothe breathe

B **1** Though my mother and her three brothers think they're healthy, they're not.

2 I thought the weather on Thursday was thoroughly threatening.

C **1** Six thick thistle sticks.

2 The other bathing brothers.

3 Not these things here, but those things there.

Am I doing something wrong?

 **All groups**

✗ Making the same sound in the words 'boat' and 'both'. You are stopping the airflow, and then suddenly releasing it. You need to make a soft, continuous hiss.

✓ Start by making a long /s/ sound. Maintain the continuous hiss.

Now, gradually slide your tongue forward until the tip rests between your teeth. Keep breathing out!

You are now producing the /θ/ sound.

 **1 2 3 4 5 6 8**

✗ Making the same sound in the words 'pass' and 'path', or 'breeze' and 'breathe'.

✓ Start by making a long /s/ sound. Slowly slide your tongue forward, while continuing to breathe out.

When the tip of your tongue sits lightly between your teeth, almost level with the lips, you will produce the correct /θ/ sound.

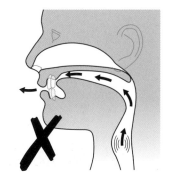

 **1 2 4 6**

✗ Making the same sound in the words 'free' and 'three'.

✓ Look in a mirror when you are practising this sound. Focus on relaxing your lips, and keeping them completely still. For /f/, your bottom lip will move, but for /θ/ it should not.

Then follow the instructions in the *Make the sounds* section, making sure that it is your tongue and teeth making the sound, not your lips and teeth.

11

SHINE & TREASURE /ʃ/ (shine), /ʒ/ (treasure)

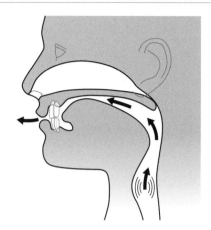

Make the sounds

DVD

1 Make a /s/ sound, as in 'soon' (see page 28).

2 Slightly round your lips.

3 Slowly slide your tongue backwards, into your mouth, just a little!

5 The sound you produce can be voiced /ʒ/ or voiceless /ʃ/ (see page 15).

When do I use this sound?

42

Voiced/voiceless	Spelling	Examples	Frequency
voiceless	sh	show, fashion, brush	often
voiceless	s	sugar	sometimes
voiceless	ss	issue	sometimes
voiceless	ti	information	sometimes
voiceless	c	ocean	sometimes
voiced	s	measure, leisure	sometimes

! The voiced sound /ʒ/ never starts an English word, but it may be heard at the beginning of *loan* words from other languages like French (e.g. 'gite', 'jus').

> **Evolving sound**
>
> In the past, words with a *ss* spelling, were pronounced with a *syoo* /sjuː/ sound, rather than *shoo* /ʃuː/. This sound is gradually changing, at different rates in different words. So you may hear words like 'issue' being pronounced in two different ways. In general, the *syoo* /sjuː/ pronunciation is more old-fashioned.

Now try it!

Say each of these words and sentences aloud. Then compare your pronunciation with the model on tracks 43–45.

A **1** <u>sh</u>oe   <u>sh</u>e   pre<u>ss</u>ure   poten<u>ti</u>al   me<u>sh</u>   pu<u>sh</u>

    2 mea<u>s</u>ure   illu<u>s</u>ion   explo<u>s</u>ion   vi<u>s</u>ion   clo<u>s</u>ure   A<u>s</u>ia

B **1** On that occasion, she was in a rush to push her way into the shop.

    2 Should we put pressure on the politician to find a solution to the situation?

    3 Affection and emotion can't be measured, but they should be treasured.

C **1** She sells seashells on the seashore.

    2 Measure huge shiny treasures.

Am I doing something wrong?

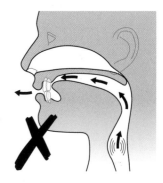

✗ Making the same sound in the words 'she' and 'see'.

✓ Start from the /s/ position (see page 28), and slowly slide your tongue backward into your mouth a little.

Slightly round your lips.

Practise moving quickly between the two sounds, trying to make them very different from each other.

✗ Making the same sound in the words 'measure' and 'mesh'.

✓ First, revise the exercises for how to make voiced and voiceless sounds (page 7).

Then, revise the *When do I use this sound?* table above for /ʃ/ and /ʒ/.

Keep a hand on your larynx while you practise, and check whether you are adding vibration or not.

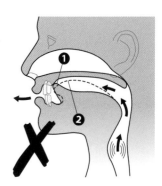

✗ Making the same sound in the words 'shoe' and 'chew'. Your tongue will move when you say /tʃ/, but it should not when you say /ʃ/.

✓ Be careful not to move your tongue until the sound is finished. Don't let your tongue tip touch the alveolar ridge. The blade of the tongue should be close to the alveolar ridge, but never touching.

12

LOVE

/l/

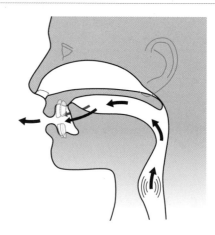

Make the sound

DVD

1   Put your tongue tip on the alveolar ridge.

2   Drop the sides of your tongue, so that they are not touching your teeth. To check this: breathe in, and you should feel cold air on the sides of your tongue.

3   Breathe out. Don't let any air out of your nose!

4   Keep your tongue in this position for the duration of this sound.

5   This sound is always voiced.

When do I use this sound?

46

Spelling	Examples	Frequency
l before a vowel	look, talent	often
ll before a vowel	caller, tallest	often

!   There are two types of /l/ – the dark and the light. The one in this unit is the light /l/, and the dark /ɫ/ is covered in the next unit (see page 40). For the rules about when to use each one, go to the next unit.

Now try it!

Say each of these words and sentences aloud. Then compare your pronunciation with the model on tracks 47–49.

A l̠isten   l̠ook   l̠emon   al̠ong   unl̠ess   fol̠l̠ow   l̠il̠y   l̠ock

B **1** The lonely lady has finally fallen in love.

2 All of the lemon trees are full of lots of fruit.

3 If you're looking for the club, take the last road on the left.

C **1** Larry's letter will arrive later.

2 Red lolly, yellow lolly. Red lolly, yellow lolly.

Am I doing something wrong?

 **2 3 4 5 6 7 8**

✗ Putting your tongue tip somewhere other than your alveolar ridge.

✓ Be sure that your tongue tip is on the alveolar ridge behind your teeth; not touching your teeth, and not curling too far backwards behind the alveolar ridge.

  4 7 8

✗ Making the same sound in the words 'look' and 'fall'. Do not lift the back of your tongue when you're making the 'look' sound. The kind of /ɫ/ used in 'fall' is described on the next page.

✓ The back of your tongue should be relaxed and low in your mouth. Check that your tongue tip is in the correct position. Then make an /l/ sound whilst yawning. This will give you the correct position for the back of the tongue. Practise keeping the back of your tongue in that position without the yawn.

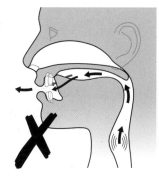

  1

✗ Making the same sound in the words 'lock' and 'rock'. If you are making this mistake your tongue is probably close to the alveolar ridge but not actually touching it.

✓ The tongue tip needs to be touching the alveolar ridge when you make this /l/ sound. The air is released sideways over the edges of the tongue unlike other tongue tip sounds.

If you are doing it correctly, you should be able to repeat 'lily, lily, lily' quite quickly. You would not be able to do this if the back of your tongue is lifting.

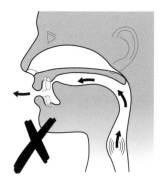

13

HILL

/ɬ/

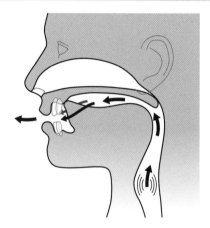

Make the sound

DVD

1 Put your tongue tip on the alveolar ridge.

2 At the same time, raise the back of your tongue to close to your soft palate. Your whole tongue will feel high in your mouth.

3 Do not touch your teeth with the sides of your tongue.

4 This sound is always voiced.

When do I use this sound?

50

Spelling	Examples	Frequency
l before a consonant	child, help	often
ll at end of a word	will, all	often
l as final sound in word	single, angle	often

! There is a silent *l* in some common words like 'walk', 'calm', and 'half'.

> **The *l* rules**
>
> The spelling rules above show that we use the dark /ɬ/ sound if the *l* is not followed by a vowel sound, either before a consonant or at the end of the word. However, if the next word starts with a vowel sound, we use the light /l/, (e.g. 'fall over', 'call off').

Now try it!

Say each of these words and sentences aloud. Then compare your pronunciation with the model on tracks 51–53.

A   be_l_t   fi_l_m   she_ll_s   wi_ll_   ru_l_e   fi_l_e   a_l_ways

B   **1**   I'll call them on my mobile when the film ends.

    2   All the children in the school felt that his rules were awful.

    3   The real result of the poll was a total fail.

C   **1**   All right, all wrong. We'll right all wrongs.

    2   Bubble gum, bubble gum – we'll gobble the bubble gum!

Am I doing something wrong?

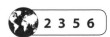

    ✗   Making a light /l/ as in 'love', when you need a dark /ɫ/ as in 'hill'. This happens when you raise only the front of your tongue, and not the back. You may be raising the back of your tongue a little, but not high enough!

    ✓   Try this exercise:

    1   Make some /g/ sounds. This will raise the back of your tongue.

    2   Keep the back of your tongue where it is, raised high towards your soft palate, and keep your lips relaxed.

    3   Then raise your tongue tip up to your alveolar ridge, keeping the back of your tongue in the /g/ position.

    4   You should now be making a dark /ɫ/.

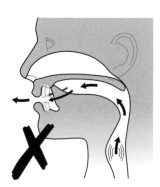

    ✗   Making a sound similar to /w/, as in 'week'. This happens if you round your lips too much.

    ✓   Relax your lips. Use a mirror, and watch your mouth as you make this sound.

    If your lips move at all, hold the corners of your lips with your fingertips, to stop them from moving.

14

HELLO

/h/

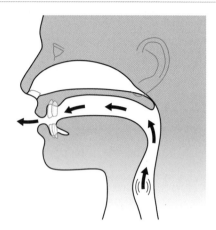

Make the sounds

DVD

1 Relax your tongue, so that it lies down in the bottom of your mouth.
2 Relax your lips into a neutral position.
3 Let out a puff of breath. Imagine that you are trying to steam up a mirror.
4 This sound is always unvoiced.

When do I use this sound?

54

Spelling	Examples	Frequency
h	hello, forehead	often
wh	who	sometimes

! Sometimes the *h* is silent, as in 'honest' and 'hour'.

Now try it!

Say each of these words and sentences aloud. Then compare your pronunciation with the model on tracks 55–57.

55–57

A help   home   behave   whole   perhaps   unhealthy

B 1 He hopes Henry's healthy and happy now.
   2 Who can help me with my hard homework?
   3 I hate to admit it, but I ate half of the ham, and the whole pot of houmous.

C 1 In Hartford, Hereford and Hampshire, hurricanes hardly ever happen.
   2 Hurry, Harry! Hurry, Harry! Harry, hurry up!

Am I doing something wrong?

✗   Raising the back of your tongue, making a hissing sound in the back of your mouth. If you are doing this, you will feel a slight tickle on the back of your tongue.

✓   Try this exercise:

1   Try to yawn, or imagine that you are opening your mouth wide for the dentist. You will feel a lot of space in your mouth, above your tongue.

2   Now exhale strongly, and you will hear a different kind of sound, from your throat. This is the /**h**/ sound of RP pronunciation.

3   You won't need to open your mouth so wide to make the sound; this is just to help you practise the sound. But you will always need to drop the back of your tongue very low.

✗   Missing out the /**h**/ sound, so that the words 'hate' and 'eight' sound the same.

✓   Get very close to a mirror, and practise breathing out so that your breath steams it up.

You should be able to hear your breath leaving your mouth. This is the /**h**/ sound.

✗   Adding a /**h**/ sound where it doesn't belong, especially before a vowel sound.

✓   Be careful not to add a /**h**/ sound if it isn't written on the page. Check by putting a hand in front of your mouth and saying the following pairs of words. You should feel a strong puff of air on your hand when you say the first word, but no puff of air for the second.

1   hair   air
2   hate   eight
3   high   eye
4   howl   owl

15

YES

/j/

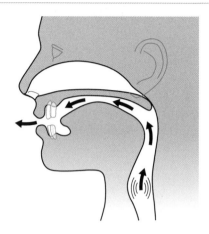

Make the sound

DVD

1   Raise your tongue towards the roof of your mouth.

2   Raise the middle of your tongue as high as possible, without actually touching the hard palate.

3   Let the sides of your tongue rest on your back teeth.

4   The long sound you make might feel (and sound) like the vowel sound in SHEEP /iː/ (see page 60).

5   This sound is always voiced.

When do I use this sound?

58

Spelling	Examples	Frequency
y before a vowel	yes, yellow	often
u at the start of a word	use, unit, unite	sometimes

The liquid /juː/

/j/ is often inserted when you don't see it in the spelling. This happens between consonants and /uː/ sounds (see page 72), in words like 'beauty', 'music', 'enthusiastic', and 'few'.

!   But there are some exceptions. Don't use the liquid /j/:

• in words with *o, oo* or *ou* in the spelling (e.g. 'move', 'boot', 'soup')

• after an /l/ (e.g. 'lunatic', 'glue', 'clue', 'blue')

• after an /r/ (e.g. 'rude', 'true')

• after /tʃ/ or /dʒ/ sounds (e.g. 'chew', 'juice').

!   *y* on the end of a word is pronounced as a vowel (e.g. 'cry', 'happy', 'boy')

Now try it!

Say each of these words and sentences aloud. Then compare your pronunciation with the model on tracks 59–61.

59–61

A   yes   you   unite   unit   reuse   cute   Tuesday

B   **1**   Did you notice the university students were very young?

      2   You wore your usual yellow dress yesterday, didn't you?

      3   To stay youthful, you should unite with your friends, listen to music, and do yoga.

C   **1**   Unique New York, unique New York.

      2   Jen is jealous of your yellow yo-yo.

Am I doing something wrong?

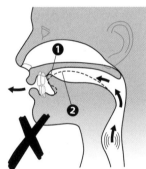

✗   Making the same sound in the words 'juice' and 'use'.

✓   Make sure that the tongue tip does not rise up to touch the alveolar ridge.

The tongue tip should be relaxed and not touching anything. It is the middle of the tongue that rises towards the hard palate.

✗   Missing out the /j/ sound, or not making it strongly enough.

✓   Practise making a separate strong /j/ sound.

Once you feel comfortable with the sound, go back and do the *Now try it!* section above.

16

WEEK

/w/

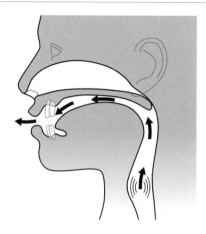

Make the sound

DVD

1 Start by making an /uː/ vowel as in GOOSE (see page 72).

2 Quickly spread and part your lips, moving the corners towards your ears.

3 Let this movement spring you into the next vowel sound in the word.

4 This sound is always voiced.

When do I use this sound?

62

Spelling	Examples	Frequency
w	want, will, fewer	often
wh	what, why, when	often
o	once, one	rarely
qu (+/k/)	quite, queen	sometimes

! w on the end of a word is pronounced as a vowel (e.g. 'grow', 'few', 'allow').

You only hear the /w/ consonant before a vowel sound.

Now try it!

Say each of these words and sentences aloud. Then compare your pronunciation with the model on tracks 63–65.

63–65 **A**

where	why	wonder	quit	queen	quiet
which	want	wish	quiz	quite	quote

B **1** I wonder why they were walking so quickly.

2 We washed the clothes we were wearing this week with warm water.

3 We wanted some peace and quiet so we quit our jobs, stopped working and travelled the world.

C Whether the weather is cold, whether the weather is hot, we'll weather the weather, whatever the weather, whether we like it or not.

Am I doing something wrong?

 **3 4 6 8**

X Making the words 'vet and 'wet' sound the same. This happens if you bring the bottom lip and teeth close together, rather than bringing the two lips together.

✓ Use a mirror to check the shape of your lips for this sound. Your lips should look round, rather than long and thin.

To correct the sound, make a small, round hole between your lips. The hole should be small enough to fit tightly around your first finger.

Use this shape to help you quickly spread and part your lips, and spring into the next sound.

Consonant clusters

When two or more consonants are next to each other, they form a consonant cluster. Consonant clusters can be tricky to pronounce for native and non-native speakers alike.

Clusters often get reduced, with one or more of the sounds either getting missed out, or changing to become very similar to the sounds next to it. This is okay in some places:

- *fths* clusters may lose the *f*, so 'fifths' becomes /fɪθs/.
- *nds* clusters may lose the *d*, so 'sends' becomes /senz/.
- *cts* clusters may lose the *t*, so 'rejects' becomes /riːdʒeks/.

Be particularly careful of consonant clusters that start with *s*, like:

- *str* strict, strange, strong
- *scr* screen, scratch, scream
- *sp* speak, Spain, spill
- *sl* slow, slip, sleep

Some people, especially Spanish speakers, will be tempted to add an /e/ sound before the first *s*. You might feel like you are sliding into the word, whispering or hissing your way onto the first sound, rather than announcing the word's arrival with a nice, definite vowel. But don't do it!

17

ROCK

/ɹ/

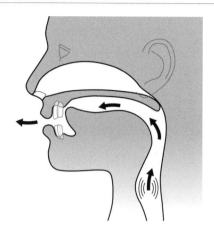

Make the sound

DVD

1 Make a /d/ sound, as in DO (see page 18).

2 As your tongue tip drops at the end of the sound, curl it back a little.

3 The tongue tip will feel like it is rising upwards towards the roof of your mouth. This is the correct position to produce the /ɹ/ sound.

4 This sound is always voiced.

When do I use this sound?

66

Spelling	Examples	Frequency
r	red, around	often
rr	carrot, purring	often
wr	write	sometimes
rh	rhythm	rarely

> **The silent r**
>
> In RP, not every r is pronounced. Many of them are silent. Missing them out is a very important part of the accent. It also has an effect on lots of the surrounding vowel sounds (that's why each vowel has its own unit). You will find an explanation of *The spoken and the silent r* in the next unit, on page 50.

Now try it!

Say each of these words and sentences aloud. Then compare your pronunciation with the model on tracks 67–69.

67–69

A

red	really	write	children	orange	arrive
round	reason	wrong	clearest	promise	current

B　**1**　Did you realize the reason he was ringing?

　　2　The crazy guitarist was wearing a green raincoat with orange carrots on it.

　　3　It's unrealistic to try to write the reference by tomorrow.

C　**1**　Rex ran round the wet rocks.

　　2　Red lorry, yellow lorry. Red lorry, yellow lorry.

Am I doing something wrong?

 2 3 4 5 6 7 8

✗　Quickly flicking the tongue tip onto the alveolar ridge and then off again. This is called a 'tapped *r*' and is the standard pronunciation for *r* in many languages, but it is never used in RP.

✓　Make sure that your tongue tip doesn't move during this sound: it should stay in one place. You should be able to prolong this sound. You can't prolong the sound if you are making a tapped *r*.

Practise the *Make the sound* section again and don't let your tongue tip hit your alveolar ridge.

 2 5 6

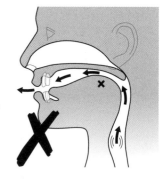

✗　Using the back of your tongue to make this sound. The back of your tongue may be pulling up and back, close to your soft palate.

✓　This sound is made with the front of your tongue, not the back.

Relax the back of your tongue, then focus on raising the front of your tongue when you make this sound.

 2 6

✗　Using your lips to help form this sound.

✓　Use a mirror to check whether your lips are moving when you make this sound.

If your lips are moving forward, hold them still with your fingers, and practise using just your tongue.

Next, remove your fingers and keep making the sound. Keep watching yourself in a mirror to make sure that your lips don't join in.

 1

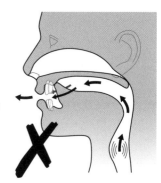

✗　Making the same sound in the words 'lock' and 'rock'.

✓　To make the / ɹ / sound, your tongue tip shouldn't touch your alveolar ridge. Drop your tongue tip down, away from the alveolar ridge.

You should feel the tip of the tongue rising and curling upwards.

Leave your tongue tip floating in your mouth, without touching anything.

18

The spoken and the silent *r*

In RP, the accent that this book uses as its model, not every *r* that is written on a page will be pronounced. This section explains when to say the *r* with an /ɹ/ and, importantly, when *not* to.

As a general rule, you should only say an /ɹ/ if the written *r* is followed by a vowel sound. This means *r* will be pronounced in words like:

70

r̲ight	r̲ed	alr̲ight	ar̲ound	near̲est
br̲ight	tr̲ust	childr̲en	ar̲row	r̲hyme

The *r* is silent if it is *not* followed by a vowel. For example, if it is…

71

- at the end of a word:

  near   four   car   fur   clear

- followed by a silent *e*:

  more   there   share   fire   pure

- followed by a consonant sound:

  force   nurse   argue   start   burn

  work   heard   girl   warm

Now try it!

In the sentences below, every *r* is silent. Practise saying each sentence aloud. You should not hear any *r* sounds, or feel your tongue lifting to make the sound.

72

1   The nurse started to cure the four men of their diseases.

2   I'm super thirsty. Please pour me some more water.

3   Did you park the car near here, or did you park it over there?

4   Did you ever tell your manager that you got here so early?

The linking /ɹ/

It is never that simple of course. If *r* is the last letter in a word, *and* the next word you are saying begins with a vowel sound, you *do* pronounce the *r* to help you link the two words.

Look at the table below. The words in the left-hand column have a silent *r* at the end. But when they are followed by a word starting with a vowel sound an /ɹ/ sound appears in the pronunciation. They are marked here in bold.

73

far	/fɑː/	far away	/fɑːɹəweɪ/
there	/ðeə/	there is	/ðeəɹɪz/
clear	/klɪə/	clear up	/klɪəɹʌp/
never	/nevə/	never again	/nevəɹəgen/

The intrusive /ɹ/

Also, native speakers will often insert an extra /ɹ/ between two vowel sounds to help them link more smoothly. This happens even when *r* is not written on the page! It is usually when the first word ends with what is called an *open* vowel, for example the sound /ə/ as in LETTER (page 54) or the /ɔː/ as in THOUGHT (page 76). Look at the table below.

74

saw	/sɔː/	saw ʳit	/sɔːɹɪt/
India	/ɪndɪə/	India ʳis	/ɪndɪəɹɪz/
awe	/ɔː/	awe ʳinspiring	/ɔːɹɪnspʌɪəɹɪŋ/

| For a quick reference guide to when to pronounce the /ɹ/ sound and when to leave it out, go to Appendix 2 on page 144. |

Now try it!

75

1   Play the audio and listen for:

- silent *r* in grey

- linking /ɹ/ sound marked with a ⌢

- and intrusive /ɹ/ sounds which are <u>underlined</u> and indicated with a small ʳ.

| Whenever⌢I hear salsa ʳor flamenco music, I always remember the year⌢I spent travelling in Latin America, India ʳand China. Have you ever heard this story? One evening, I was singing and dancing with Joanna ʳand Sarah, and as I journeyed home I saw ʳa glitzy media ʳevent taking place at the other⌢end of town. It looked as though things were drawʳing to a close, so I thought I'd wander⌢in for⌢a large glass of water⌢or something. I knew I wasn't meant to be there, but suddenly there was mass hysteria ʳin the room. It was clear⌢I'd done something very wrong when I was formally arrested by the police officer. Even after⌢all the drama ʳended, I'll still never⌢understand why it was so serious. But I learnt my lesson, and I'll never⌢again go to a party, unless I'm certain I'm invited! |

76

2   Now have a go yourself. Before you listen to the second recording, mark the text using the symbols in the same way as above (you can cross out the silent *r*). Then play the audio and see if you were correct.

| The giant panda is definitely our favourite animal. We love their amazing faces, and black and white colouring. Pandas are extremely fond of eating bamboo, and you'll often find them with their paw on a bamboo plant! Unfortunately, the panda is an endangered species, which means there aren't as many of them around as there used to be. You're unlikely ever to see a panda in the wild – in order to do that, you'd have to become an explorer and travel to China on holiday. China is the only country where any pandas live outside captivity. And you won't find them in every area of China as they're only in Western areas. I wonder if I'd have to arrange a visa in order to go to China. I'm sure it'd be worth it! |

You can check the correct marking on page 146.

The vowel sounds

Vowels are open sounds. That means there is no contact between your articulators while you make the sound; your tongue and lips don't touch each other or anything else. This is different from the consonant sounds where there is always an obstruction to the airflow, by the lips or by the tongue. You should be able to create the shape of a vowel and sustain it for as long as you want. You change from one vowel to another by moving your lips and tongue.

Because vowel sounds have no contact points in the mouth it can be harder to feel how your articulators make the sounds. But you do need to learn this in order to create the vowels accurately and consistently. Start by working in front of a mirror so that you can be confident that you are shaping the sounds accurately. You may be surprised to find that what you are actually doing is not the same as what you think you are doing.

Monophthongs and diphthongs

There are two different kinds of vowel: *Monophthongs* (see pages 54–77) and *Diphthongs* (see pages 81–88).

A monophthong is only one sound (*mono* means one) so your lips and tongue do not move at all during the sound and it is the same sound from the beginning to the end. For example, in the word 'sheep', the /iː/ made by the *ee* is a monophthong.

There are two types of monophthong: those with long sounds and those with shorter sounds. Each unit will tell you if the sound is long or short. But, in general, there will always be a mix of long and short sounds in anything you say, and your speech will be filled with contrasts between the two.

The prefix *di* means two so the *diphthongs* contain two different sounds. They require your lips and tongue to move from one sound into the other. This is explained in a lot more detail in *An introduction to diphthongs* (pages 78–80).

Shaping the vowel sounds

Look at the diagram on the next page. You can use it to help shape your vowel sounds.

On the left-hand side of the grid are the sounds with very widely spread lips, and on the right are the sounds with very strongly rounded lips.

At the top of the grid are sounds with the least space above your tongue, and at the bottom are sounds with the most space above your tongue.

The shapes in the four corners of the grid are the most extreme shapes possible and none of these are used to make RP vowel sounds. This grid will help you to understand how the mouth shapes for all the sounds relate to each other.

In the *Make the sound* section of each unit, you will see a 'grid reference' – this number shows you where on the chart that vowel goes. It will help you to learn exactly how your mouth should look, in relation to the other vowels around it, in order to get the mouth position exactly right.

Vowel positioning diagram

Openness

Spreading

More tips for using the vowels section

Apart from the additional reference to the *Vowel positioning diagram*, the sounds in the vowel units are presented in a similar way to the consonants, with a *Make the sound, When do I use this sound?* and *Now try it!* section for each. There is also an *Am I doing something wrong?* section, but it is not distinguished by language region because most learners tend to make similar errors, regardless of their native language.

As before, remember to use a mirror (see page 4 on mirror practice) and to record yourself speaking the sound so you can listen back.

Vowels are strongly affected by the sounds around them as they glide from one to another so the shape of a vowel may alter slightly depending on what comes before or after. First practise the sounds on their own, and then build up to words and sentences.

Vowels can be particularly confusing to non-native speakers of English because the spellings can be varied and often misleading. When you are working through these units, try to aim for consistency with each sound, regardless of the spelling.

19

LETT**ER**, COMM**A** /ə/

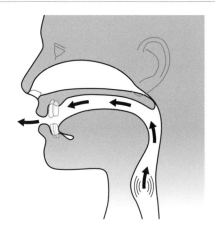

This sound is called the **schwa**, but it is also known as the **neutral vowel**. It is an essential vowel sound in creating good English rhythm, and is arguably the most important sound you will learn in English. Because of this there are specific units devoted to it in the *RP rhythm* section of this book (Units 48–52). Use this unit to learn how to create the schwa. Use the *RP rhythm* section to learn in more detail when to use it.

Make the sound

Vowel grid reference: 5

This vowel is short.

DVD

1 Part your lips and teeth, just a little.

2 Relax your tongue and leave the tip to rest naturally, just behind your bottom front teeth.

3 Now make a very short sound.

4 The schwa should have no shape at all. Lips, tongue and jaw are all neutral and relaxed.

When do I use this sound?

The schwa can replace any spelt vowel in an unstressed syllable or word. The rules are covered in detail in on pages 110–111.

77

Spelling	Examples
a	around, comma
e	begin, other
i	possible
o	official, director
u	particular

Now try it!

Say each of these words and sentences aloud. Then compare your pronunciation with the model on tracks 78–79.

78–79

A

Pet**er**	sev**en**	lett**er**	oth**er**	comput**er**	fam**ous**
particul**ar**	anoth**er**	f**or**get	glam**our**	inf**or**mation	**a**musing

B **1** Her mother opened the letter that was addressed to her father.

  2 The bananas were a peculiar colour but Debra ate them anyway.

  3 Her new dietician was stricter than she expected and though she wasn't supposed to eat after seven, hunger got the better of her.

Am I doing something wrong?

✗ A common mistake is to try and shape this vowel based on its spelling in the written word.

✓ If you use the schwa correctly, it should not be possible to guess how the word is spelt when you hear it. The schwa is completely neutral. It can almost disappear in speech. You might find it useful to imagine the spelling of your target word without a vowel at all:

e.g.   control   =   c'ntrol

banana   =   b'nana

television   =   tel'vis'n

---

s and *es* plural endings

When you make a word plural or possessive by adding *s*, sometimes this is pronounced /s/ or /z/ and sometimes /ɪz/.

- You add the vowel sound /ɪ/ before the /z/ if the original word ends in:

  /s/   glass ➔ glasses /glɑːsɪz/

  /ʃ/   bush ➔ bushes /bʊʃɪz/

  /z/   maze ➔ mazes /meɪzɪz/

  /tʃ/   bench ➔ benches /bentʃɪz/

  /dʒ/   edge ➔ edges /edʒɪz/

  Just add the /s/ or /z/, without the extra vowel, for all other words:

  words /wɜːdz/   bins /bɪnz/   cars /kɑːz/   stops /stɒps/   Tim's /tɪmz/

ed endings for the past tense

When you put a verb into the past tense by adding *ed*, sometimes this is pronounced just as a /t/ or /d/ (e.g. ask**ed**), and sometimes with a vowel sound /ɪd/ (e.g. want**ed**).

- If the original verb already ends with *t* or *d*, you need to add the extra vowel:

  waited /weɪtɪd/   ended /endɪd/   shouted /ʃæʊtɪd/   wanted /wɒntɪd/

- All other words just use the consonant sounds *t* or *d*:

  waved /weɪvd/   wished /wɪʃt/   raced /ɹeɪst/   laughed /lɑːft/

20

NURSE

/ɜː/

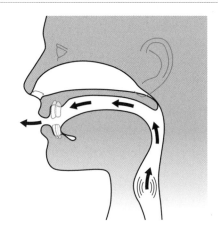

Make the sound

Vowel grid reference: 6

This vowel is a longer version of the schwa (see page 54) with a slightly lower tongue position.

DVD

1 Part your lips and teeth, just a little.

2 Relax your tongue and leave the tip to rest naturally just behind your bottom front teeth; the tongue should be a fraction lower than for the /ə/ sound.

3 Now make a long vowel sound.

4 Don't allow the tongue to move or the lips to make a shape – however tempting! Lips, tongue and jaw are all neutral and relaxed.

When do I use this sound?

This sound is always spelt with a silent *r*. Never pronounce an /ɹ/; only pronounce the vowel sound.

80

Spelling	Examples
ur	urgent, fur, curse
er	eternity, nervous, commercial
ir	bird, girl, virtue
ear	early, learn, heard
or	work, word, worst
our	journey, courteous, journalist

Now try it!

Say each of these words and sentences aloud. Then compare your pronunciation with the model on tracks 81–83.

81–83

A w<u>or</u>ld   w<u>or</u>d   <u>jour</u>ney   c<u>our</u>tesy   t<u>ur</u>n   st<u>ir</u>   c<u>er</u>tain

n<u>er</u>ve   g<u>ir</u>l   b<u>ir</u>d   sk<u>ir</u>t   s<u>ear</u>ch   <u>ear</u>th   h<u>ear</u>d

B **1** She urged him to curse less as she yearned for a perfect and virtuous partner.

2 The circus clowns wore purple shirts and juggled thirty burning balls, making the front row of the audience very nervous.

3 She turned up early to her first day of work to be certain of the perfect first impression.

C <u>Birds</u>
Have you ever heard the saying 'the early bird catches the worm'? It means that whoever gets to an opportunity first is most likely to do well. Birds do eat worms, and they also certainly do wake up early in the morning and start chirping and singing! Certain birds make massive journeys every year, migrating from cold to warm climates. This seems like very hard work; some fly almost half-way around the Earth. Bird watchers like to observe the times of these birds' journeys, and search for them when they arrive at their destination. Of course, not all birds travel like this. Some birds, like turkeys, can't even fly at all.

Am I doing something wrong?

This vowel is difficult for all students whatever their native language and these notes and exercises will be helpful for all learners.

In RP this long sound is always spelt with a silent *r*, and many learners will try to pronounce the *r* in some way. This makes the vowel sound seem shorter and less open (see pages 50–51 on *The spoken and the silent* r). Try the exercise below:

Look at this sentence:

> She was so nervous she woke up early and took the purse that matched her perfect white shirt and black skirt outfit to work on her first day at the law firm.

Now let's change each *r* that we don't pronounce to grey:

> She was so nervous she woke up early and took the purse that matched her perfect white shirt and black skirt outfit to work on her first day at the law firm.

Look how much space is created in the words. Imagine that space is time that you can add on to the vowel sound. Don't say the *r*, but use the space to create a longer, more open vowel.

First, read the grey *r* sentence in front of the mirror. Don't think about the meaning, just think about shape. Go very slowly, and check that on each **/ɜː/** word you are making the same vowel shape.

Speed up, check again and record yourself if you want.

This vowel can feel very non-specific to some learners. Like the schwa, it is a neutral vowel – you do nothing with your mouth to make it. The idea of not shaping the sound can be hard to match with the various spellings used.

Think of it like this instead: this vowel *does* have a shape, but it's a very central shape. A way to learn the shape is to glide from the vowel sound in BATH (see page 68) to the vowel sound in SHEEP (see page 60). You will find the NURSE vowel in the middle of that slide. You can come back to this sound when you've had a chance to practise those other sounds if you like.

21

KIT

/ɪ/

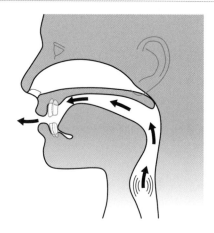

Make the sound

Vowel grid reference: 1

This vowel is short.

DVD

1 Part your lips and drop the lower jaw a little.

2 Relax your tongue and allow the tip to rest just behind your bottom front teeth. If you look in a mirror, you should be able to see the middle of the tongue move up and forward.

3 The lips do not need to spread for this sound, but some speakers do spread their lips slightly, and that's okay.

When do I use this sound?

84

Spelling	Examples
i	in, sit, pick
a + ge	village, cabbage, manage
y	myth, hymn, symbol
ui	building, biscuit

There is also a table with examples of when this sound is found in unstressed syllables in the appendix on page 143.

Now try it!

Say each of these words and sentences aloud. Then compare your pronunciation with the model on tracks 85–87.

85–87

A ship   bit   split   women   village   rubbish   manage

trick   building   dish   hymn   him   silly   hill

B **1** Bill did the dishes while Milly nibbled biscuits on the picnic blanket in the middle of their big garden.

2 It would have been simpler if we'd picked a different route. This one is a little hilly.

3 The incredibly big ship was sinking into the tiny little river, so luckily it was a silly sight instead of a disastrous one.

C Pigs

A typical pig has a big head, hooved toes and a massive snout which they use to dig into soil to find food. Pigs are omnivores who eat plants and animals though these days in captivity they are fed a diet of special feed enriched with vitamins and minerals. Domestic pigs have become quite popular, and the pot-bellied pig is the celebrity favourite of the moment. If you call someone 'a pig', it suggests that they are dirty or a bit messy, probably because pigs like to roll in mud to keep cool, but in actual fact pigs are very clean.

Am I doing something wrong?

✗ Many speakers will swap this vowel for its similar, longer partner /iː/, making the same sound in the words 'kit' and 'sheep'.

✓ Lower the tongue slightly. Check in the mirror that you aren't pushing the sides of the tongue against the top molars. Always remember to keep this vowel short.

Watch the DVD to see and hear the difference between the two sounds.

Try these exercises:

1 In a mirror, try swapping between the SHEEP and KIT vowels quickly. Look for the movement of your tongue.

eeeee–i–eeeee–i–eeeee–i–eeeee–i–eeeee–i

iː   ɪ   iː   ɪ   iː   ɪ   iː   ɪ   iː   ɪ

88

Then compare your own sound to the one on the audio track.

2 Now try swapping between some words which have the vowel sounds, like 'sheep' and 'kit' or:

green–bit   green–bit   green–bit

been–bin   been–bin   been–bin

Then compare your own pronunciation to the speaker on the audio track.

Keep repeating these until you are able to place the correct vowel sound.

✗ Some speakers spread the lips too much. The lips should only be very slightly spread.

✓ Check in a mirror to see that your lips are in the correct grid position (see page 53). Remember, what you think you are doing and what you are actually doing may be different.

22

SH**EE**P

/iː/

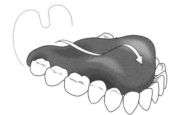
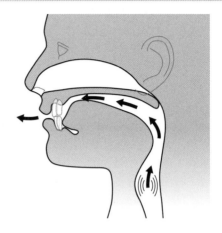

Make the sound

Vowel grid reference: 1

This vowel is long.

DVD

1 The jaw is slightly open.

2 Relax your tongue and allow the tip to rest just behind your bottom front teeth. If you look in a mirror, you should be able to see the middle of the tongue move strongly up and forward.

3 The sides of the tongue should push lightly against the top teeth.

4 The lips do not need to spread for this sound, but some speakers do spread their lips slightly, and that's okay.

When do I use this sound?

89

Spelling	Examples
e	me, he, evil
ea	each, pea, sea
ee	speed, needy
ie	grieve, belief
ei	receive
i	police
y on the ends of words (NB: this sound is slightly shorter)	happy, money

! In older pronunciation dictionaries, y on the end of a word can be written as an /ɪ/.

Now try it!

Say each of these words and sentences aloud. Then compare your pronunciation with the model on tracks 90–92.

90–92

A me   she   pl_ea_se   qu_ay_   l_ea_f   m_ea_n   cr_ea_sed   b_ea_d

key   t_ea_   ind_ee_d   s_ee_d   gr_ie_f   bel_ie_ve   conc_ei_ve   pol_i_ce

B **1** He seems to me to be mean, and really creepy. What does she see in him?

2 She didn't believe she was speeding, and was annoyed the policeman took away her keys.

3 Sweet cream and berries are very pleasing indeed at teatime.

C Sheep

Sheep are normally raised for their fleece, meat, milk and, in some regions, cheese. Sheep is the word used for both a single animal and a group of them, which can seem a little confusing to international speakers keen to distinguish between 'these sheep' and 'this sheep'.

There are many breeds of domestic sheep with the most common being a white colour. Sheep eat green leaves, grass and seeds. They eat most quickly in the morning as they digest their food later in the day. They seem quite timid and tend to flee any situation they find scary, but they are really very intelligent animals.

Am I doing something wrong?

✗ Many speakers will swap this vowel for its similar, shorter partner /ɪ/, making the same sound in the words SHEEP and KIT.

✓ You can correct this mistake by slightly raising the tongue and lightly pushing the front edges of the tongue against the top teeth. Remember, don't make it too short.

Watch the DVD to see and hear the difference between the two sounds.

Try these exercises:

93

1 Learning to hear the difference between the two sounds will help you to correct this problem. You can practise the contrast from the /ɪ/ vowel sound (see page 58) if you want. Or try some new ones:

lip–leap   lip–leap   lip–leap

pick–seed   pick–seed   pick–seed

2 Learning to hear the difference between the two sounds will help you to correct this problem. Compare the two sounds in a full sentence. /iː/ as in SHEEP is the long vowel shown in CAPITALS, and /ɪ/ is the shorter vowel shown in *italics*.

Sp*EA*king *isn't* as EAsy as wE think *it is*. WE will nEEd to pract*i*se!

Notice how the vowels in *italics* seem faster and more bouncy, whilst the CAPITAL sounds are more stressed and weightier.

23

DR**E**SS

/e/

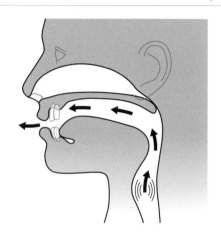

Make the sound

Vowel grid reference: 4

This vowel is short.

DVD

1   Relax your tongue and allow the tip to rest just behind your bottom front teeth.

2   Let the front of the tongue raise slightly as though it is heading for the roof of the mouth.

3   The tongue tip does not need to come up.

When do I use this sound?

94

Spelling	Examples
e	red, yes
ea	spread, head
a	many, any
ie	friend
ai	again
eo	leopard
ay	says

Now try it!

Say each of these words and sentences aloud. Then compare your pronunciation with the model on tracks 95–97.

95–97

A

separate	bed	mental	men	depend	spend	deadly
head	many	anything	said	friend	next	attend

B

1 The wedding is next Wednesday and the headdress isn't ready yet. So yes, I'm stressed!
2 They went all the way to the shopping centre for the best bread in Essex.
3 Breakfast was excellent and Ben's belly felt very full.

C Hedgehogs

As the name suggests, hedgehogs like to live in hedgerows where there's plenty of edible treats like berries and insects. If you're a nature fan there's never been a better time to explore the habitat of hedgehogs with the English summer getting warmer every year. Hedgehogs are easily recognizable because of their sharp spines, and in these they have an excellent form of defence – when they see a threat, they roll into a spiky ball.

Am I doing something wrong?

✗ Opening your mouth too wide and making the same vowel sound in the words 'trap' and 'dress'.

✓ Raise the front of your tongue slightly. Look in a mirror and compare the words 'head', 'hat'. You should see movement in the lip shape and tongue position. Look on the *Vowel positioning diagram* (page 53) and compare the shapes of these vowels.

✗ Making the same vowel sound in the words 'hair' and 'head'. If you are doing this then you are adding a small schwa sound after the /e/ and creating a diphthong (see page 78).

✓ Use a mirror to check there is no movement in the lips and tongue when you make this sound. It may be easier to practise with words that have a plosive consonant (/p/, /b/, /t/, /d/, /k/, /g/) at the end – these give more definite finishing points.

e.g.   head   bed   said   dead

✗ Making a different diphthong by adding a short /ɪ/ vowel to the start (onglide) of this vowel sound.

✓ Pick a short word with the /e/ sound (e.g. 'bed') and, using a mirror, say each sound separately and work through the word.

e.g.   b   e   d   b   e   d
       /b/ /e/ /d/   /b/ /e/ /d/

Make sure that the vowel sound /e/ is only one sound, not /ɪe/.

Now, put the word sounds back together but keep the vowel pure.

24

CAP

/æ/

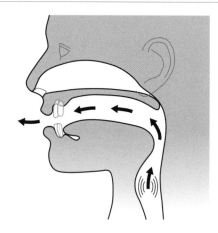

Make the sound

Vowel grid reference: 8

This vowel is short.

DVD

1   Relax your tongue and rest the tip just behind your bottom front teeth.

2   The back of the tongue is low for this sound. The blade lifts forward slightly, but not the tongue tip.

3   The tongue tip stays down low.

When do I use this sound?

98

Spelling	Examples
a	mat, angry

Now try it!

Say each of these words and sentences aloud. Then compare your pronunciation with the model on tracks 99–101.

99–101

A   c<u>a</u>t   h<u>a</u>t   m<u>a</u>tch   p<u>a</u>ttern   st<u>a</u>ndard   m<u>a</u>tter   underst<u>a</u>nd

m<u>a</u>n   f<u>a</u>t   beg<u>a</u>n   p<u>a</u>nda   m<u>a</u>gic   c<u>a</u>ndle   m<u>a</u>ndatory

B   1   I'll take the bags of cash to the bank on Saturday and grab some stamps on the way back.

2   She was so mad, she sat on his hat and then stamped on his valuable clarinet. 'Ha!' she thought.

3   He grabbed his coat but forgot his cap as he had to dash to catch the match.

C Cats

The cat has become the standard city dwellers' companion. In fact, there are thousands of cats in the UK. Cats are big fans of routine and are happiest following a regular daily pattern including lying on their owner's lap, and lapping up sunshine with a nap in the back garden. They can have some bad habits, such as scratching up furniture to sharpen their retractable claws. They are natural predators and prone to catching any wild animals that happen to wander into their garden, from rabbits to landing birds.

Am I doing something wrong?

✗ Making the same vowel sound in the words CAP and CUP. Both of these vowels are open and short so it is common for learners to confuse them.

✓ To say CAP, rather than CUP, the lips are more spread, and the tongue is slightly higher at the front.

Watch the DVD to see and hear the difference between the two sounds.

First check your lip position for both vowels using the *Vowel positioning diagram* (page 53). The /æ/ of CAP is open and wide, but the /ʌ/ of CUP is open and long.

102

1 Now, using a mirror, alternate between the two sounds:

ah–uh–ah–uh–ah–uh–ah–uh

æ ʌ æ ʌ æ ʌ æ ʌ

Make sure that you are doing a different lip position for each, and that your tongue moves slightly between the sounds.

2 Now try swapping between some words which have the sounds, like 'cap' and 'cup' or:

bat–but	bat–but	bat–but
hat–hut	hat–hut	hat–hut

Don't let the consonant sounds around the vowels change your lip shape too much.

✗ Making the same vowel sound in the words 'bad' and 'bed'. If you are doing this, then you are holding your tongue too high.

✓ Look in a mirror and compare these words.

bet–bat

met–mat

men–man

said–sad

Make sure you see the tongue rise for the words spelt with an *e* and *ai*, and drop for the words spelt with an *a*.

25

CUP

/ʌ/

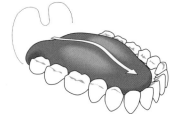

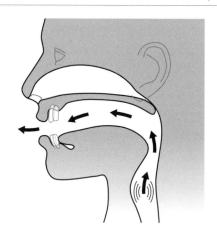

Make the sound

Vowel grid reference: 9

This vowel is short.

DVD

1 Relax your tongue, and rest the tongue tip just behind your bottom front teeth.

2 Slightly lift the middle of your tongue.

When do I use this sound?

103

Spelling	Examples
u	fun, ugly
o	love, colour
oo	blood, flooding
ou	tough, double

Now try it!

Say each of these words and sentences aloud. Then compare your pronunciation with the model on tracks 104–106.

104–106

A cut   shut   butter   hunter   must   something

stuff   money   honey   nothing   enough   flood

B

1 There's just enough butter left for one more if you want another muffin.

2 I've had enough of your worrying – trust me. It'll be fun.

3 Nothing's as yummy as this Southern honey – you'll love it!

C   Monkeys

There are dozens of different kinds of monkey. Some are small, and others are much bigger. Monkeys are closely related to humans – you could say they're our distant cousins. Sometimes when watching monkeys, we can recognize human behaviours, and it can be very funny! For example, some monkeys use tools and construct ordered societies. Scientific studies have shown that monkeys understand language and can solve problems and communicate. In some countries monkeys can be seen as pests; they sometimes gather in such large numbers that they can become quite threatening. There are stories of monkeys becoming rough and violent with members of the public. They also sometimes cause damage by munching on crops being grown on farms.

Am I doing something wrong?

✗   Making the same vowel sound in the words CUP and CAP. Both of these vowels are open and short so it is common for learners to confuse them.

✓   To say CUP, rather than CAP, the lips are less spread, and the tongue is slightly higher in the middle.

Watch the DVD to see and hear the difference between the two sounds.

First, check your lip position for both vowels using the *Vowel positioning diagram* (page 53). The /ʌ/ of CUP is open and long, but the /æ/ of CAP is open and wide.

107

1   Now, using a mirror, alternate between the two sounds:

uh–ah–uh–ah–uh–ah–uh–ah

ʌ æ ʌ æ ʌ æ ʌ æ

Make sure that you are doing a different lip position for each, and that your tongue moves slightly between the sounds.

2   Now try swapping between some words which have the sounds, like CUP and CAP or:

cut–pat	cut–pat	cut–pat
hut–cat	hut–cat	hut–cat

Don't let the sounds around the vowels change your lip shape too much.

✗   Making a sound that is too similar to the schwa (see page 54) instead of an /ʌ/.

✓   Open the mouth more, which will make the tongue feel lower.

Try the exercise below:

107a

1   The following words contain both /ʌ/ vowel sounds (in CAPITALS) and schwa vowel sounds (in *italics*). In each word the /ʌ/ vowel is stressed. Say each one in front of a mirror and make sure the /ʌ/ vowels are CLEAR AND BRIGHT, and the mouth is more open, and the schwas are *small and quick*:

*an*Other	shUdd*er*	nUmb*er*	*a*brUpt	bUtt*er*
cUstom*er*	hUndr*ed*	Utt*er*ance	*o*bstrUct	

Learning to hear the difference between the two sounds will help you to correct this problem.

26

B**A**TH

/ɑː/

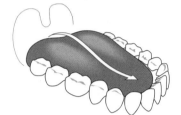
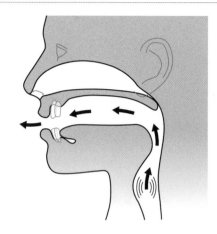

Make the sound

Vowel grid reference: 9

This vowel is long.

DVD

1   Open your mouth quite wide.

2   Relax your tongue and allow the tip to rest just behind your bottom front teeth.

3   Your tongue will feel a little lower than the NURSE sound (see page 56).

When do I use this sound?

108

Spelling	Examples
a + th, f, s, n	path, staff, photograph, class, dance
ar	start, market
ear	heart, hearth
au	laughter, auntie
al	balm

Now try it!

Say each of these words and sentences aloud. Then compare your pronunciation with the model on tracks 109–111.

109–111

A   last   car   after   path   palm   can't   dancer   rather

past   bar   start   part   aunt   calm   heart   casting

B   **1**   She started laughing at her aunt's party dancing.

2   The large palm trees swayed in the afternoon breeze.

3   The bar was very smart looking and a charming place for a glass of wine after a hard day's work.

C   Giraffes

The giraffe is a native of the grasslands and savannah between Chad, Somalia and South Africa, but there are now many in captivity. They are an animal that can inspire laughter due to their rather bizarre appearance, namely their long neck and black and tan patterned body. They aren't the fastest of animals and they can't swim, yet adult giraffes aren't targeted by many predators – only the calves are at risk.

Am I doing something wrong?

 Making the same vowel sound in the words BATH and CAP (page 64).

 The /ɑː/ vowel sound in BATH is the most open sound in RP. To find the position, look in a mirror and imagine you are an opera singer trying to hit a high note. The jaw is dropped low, the tongue is flat and low and the lips are in a long oval.

The /æ/ vowel in CAP is shorter, and the tongue is lifting slightly. Compare them on the *Vowel positioning diagram* on page 53.

Watch the DVD to see and hear the difference between the two sounds.

 Try the exercise below:

112

1   The following sentence contains both /ɑː/ vowel sounds (in CAPITALS) and /æ/ vowel sounds (in *italics*). Say the sentence, and compare the two.

Matt l*a*cked im*a*gination, so it was m*a*d of CArl to Ask him to stArt an *a*dult drAma clAss.

Learning to hear the difference between the two sounds will help you to correct the problem.

27

FOOT /ʊ/

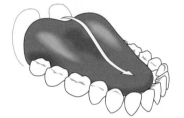

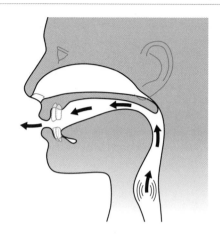

Make the sound

Vowel grid reference: 2

This vowel is short.

DVD

1 Relax your tongue and allow the tongue tip to rest just behind your bottom front teeth.

2 The back of the tongue is high for this sound.

When do I use this sound?

113

Spelling	Examples
u	put, pull, butcher
oo	foot, stood
ou	could, would, should
o	wolf

Now try it!

Say each of these words and sentences aloud. Then compare your pronunciation with the model on tracks 114–116.

114–116

A

full	pudding	pushed	sugar	good	book
wolf	hooded	could	footstep	cushion	would

B

1 This sugary pudding is full of goodness.

2 Wouldn't it be better if you looked for new wool socks?

3 Put the book on the shelf by all the other cookbooks.

C Wolves

Wolves used to be a common sight in the British countryside, but they're now extinct in the UK and wolf populations worldwide are generally on the decline. Europe used to be full of wolves, as was a good part of the United States. It was a normal sight to see large groups of wolves running through forests and woodlands. Wolves are cousins of the modern dog, and therefore look quite similar. Wolves have a strong connection with the full moon, and it often puts them in the mood to start howling. The reasons for this are not fully understood. Humans have always had an unusual relationship with wolves. There are lots of books about wolves, and references to them in folklore – like werewolves which could only be killed with a silver bullet, or the story of Little Red Riding Hood, in which a woman is eaten by a wolf. Over the years, there have been a few examples of wolves attacking humans, but it's more common for them to be a threat to livestock, such as sheep, which are farmed for their wool.

Am I doing something wrong?

✗ Making the same vowel sound in the words GOOSE and FOOT. You are probably rounding the lips too much and holding the tongue too high.

✓ Bring the back of your tongue down a little and don't push it out too far. Look on the *Vowel positioning diagram* (page 53) and compare the shapes of these vowels. The 'foot' vowel sound is shorter than the 'goose' vowel sound.

Watch the DVD to see and hear the difference between the two sounds.

Try the exercises below:

1 In a mirror, try swapping between the FOOT and GOOSE vowels quickly. Look for the movement of your tongue.

Look at the difference between the lip shapes. Feel how the back of the tongue moves slightly between each sound.

uh–ooooo–uh–ooooo–uh–ooooo–uh–ooooo–uh–ooooo

ʊ uː ʊ uː ʊ uː ʊ uː ʊ uː

Then compare your own sound to the one on the audio track.

2 Now try swapping between some words which have the sounds, like FOOT and GOOSE or:

put–who	put–who	put–who
took–two	took–two	took–two

Notice how the /uː/ is longer and stronger, whilst the /ʊ/ is light and bouncy.

3 The following sentence contains both /uː/ vowel sounds (in CAPITALS) and /ʊ/ vowel sounds (in *italics*). Say the sentence, and compare the two.

The rUde and mOOdy dUke *could* be redUced to a *pussy*cat by the *good* woman's bEAUtiful mUsic.

Learning to hear the difference between the two sounds will help you to correct the problem.

28

GOOSE /uː/

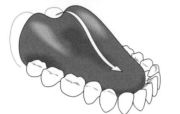

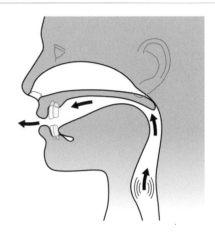

Make the sound

Vowel grid reference: 3

This vowel is long.

DVD

1 Relax your tongue and allow the tip to rest just behind your bottom front teeth.

2 The back of the tongue is very high for this sound.

When do I use this sound?

118

Spelling rule	Word example
u	nude, tuna, glue
eau	beauty
o	do, movie, shoe
oo	food, smooth
ou	youth
ew	new, few
ui	juice, bruise

Now try it!

Say each of these words and sentences aloud. Then compare your pronunciation with the model on tracks 119–121.

A t<u>u</u>be   r<u>u</u>de   tr<u>u</u>th   am<u>u</u>sing   m<u>ou</u>sse   m<u>o</u>ve   fr<u>ui</u>t

tw<u>o</u>   y<u>ou</u>   sch<u>oo</u>l   b<u>eau</u>tiful   m<u>oo</u>dy   st<u>ew</u>   gr<u>ew</u>

B **1** The cruise ship had a movie theatre and excellent food.

2 By June the tulips were blooming beautifully.

3 The new school was truly super.

C <u>Moose</u>

The moose is a huge and beautiful animal. They like cold climates, so countries that have moose include Russia, the United States and Canada. In terms of food, they don't eat meat, and prefer to chew on plants and vegetables. Male moose usually have two large antlers on their heads (which they lose before the winter). They are excellent swimmers, and are often found in pools, keeping cool. The main natural threats to moose are wolves and bears. The newest threat is humans whose cars collide with moose, often leaving them seriously wounded.

Am I doing something wrong?

✗ Making the same vowel sound in the words GOOSE and FOOT.

✓ Round your lips more, pushing them forward a little and raising the back of the tongue more.

Look on the *Vowel positioning diagram* (page 53) and compare the shapes of these vowels. The GOOSE vowel sound is also longer than the FOOT vowel sound.

Go to the exercises in the *Am I doing something wrong?* section of /ʊ/ FOOT (see page 70) to work on this.

Watch the DVD to see and hear the difference between the two sounds.

29

LOT

/ɒ/

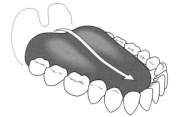

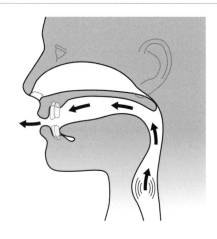

Make the sound

Vowel grid reference: 10

This vowel is short.

DVD

1 Relax your tongue and allow the tip to rest just behind your bottom front teeth.

2 The back of the tongue is low, almost as low as for /ɑː/ as in 'bath'.

When do I use this sound?

122

Spelling	Examples
o	not, gone, pottery
a	wanted, watch, quantity
ou	cough

Now try it!

Say each of these words and sentences aloud. Then compare your pronunciation with the model on tracks 123–125.

123–125

A hot shot robot cloth spotted cough

trough wrong want what washing salted

B 1 She needed lots of strong, hot coffee.

2 The boss has a lot of dodgy old documents in boxes at the office.

3 She lost her plot at the allotment and had nowhere to grow her poppies.

C   Dogs

A lot of my friends have got dogs. They're a really popular pet, because they're so loyal. There are a lot of different sorts of dogs. You can choose whatever kind of dog you want to suit your lifestyle. Some dogs are working dogs, and help humans by doing various jobs. Some work on farms, controlling sheep; others help with transport, particularly in snowy areas. It's also common for dogs to help the emergency services, or soldiers, because they have such a wonderful sense of smell.

Am I doing something wrong?

✗   Making the same vowel sound in the words LOT and CUP.

✓   Rounding your lips more. This vowel needs a rounded lip shape. Look at the *Vowel positioning diagram* (page 53) and compare the shapes of these vowels.

Use a mirror to make sure you are making the correct shape with your lips.

Watch the DVD to see and hear the difference between the two sounds.

✗   Making the same vowel sound in the words LOT and THOUGHT. This mistake is very common.

✓   The /ɒ/ vowel is short, with lips rounded a little, whilst the /ɔː/ vowel is long with lips rounded much more. Go to the exercises in the *Am I doing something wrong?* section of the /ɔː/ vowel sound (see page 77) to work on this.

Watch the DVD to see and hear the difference between the two sounds.

✗   Making the same vowel sound in the words LOT and BATH. This is due to the influence of American English on the way English is spoken around the world.

✓   Look in a mirror and use the *Vowel positioning diagram* (page 53) for the difference between these two shapes. The /ɒ/, as in LOT, has lip rounding, whereas the lips are unrounded for the /ɑː/, as in BATH.

✗   Making the vowel sound too similar to a schwa.

✓   You are not opening the mouth enough and you are not rounding the lips. Try some mouth exercises before you go on.

Make your mouth as big as you can.

Now make it as wide as you can with a huge smile.

Now think of someone you love and blow a big kiss.

Now go back to the /ɒ/ instructions and check yourself in a mirror. Make sure this sound is rounded and open enough.

30

TH**OU**GHT

/ɔː/

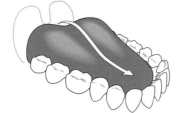

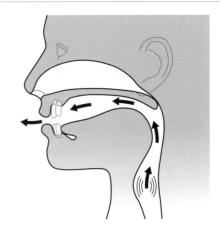

Make the sound

Vowel grid reference: 7

This vowel is long.

DVD

1 Relax your tongue and allow the tip to rest just behind your bottom front teeth.

2 The back of the tongue is high, but not as high as for the GOOSE vowel (page 72).

When do I use this sound?

126

Spelling	Examples
or	sport, north
al	walking, chalk, tall
ou	bought, source, thoughtful
au	caution, naughty
aw	law, paw

Now try it!

Say each of these words and sentences aloud. Then compare your pronunciation with the model on tracks 127–129.

127–129

A

b<u>a</u>ll	f<u>or</u>ce	t<u>al</u>king	c<u>au</u>ght	sp<u>or</u>t	<u>Au</u>gust	f<u>ou</u>r
<u>aw</u>e	c<u>our</u>se	res<u>ou</u>rce	th<u>ou</u>ght	sh<u>or</u>t	t<u>au</u>ght	w<u>al</u>k

B

1 He thought she caught the four forty train, but she boarded the fourteen forty.

2 She's awfully sporty, and spends all her time on the netball court.

3 The autumn ball was awesome, and not as boring as Paul had thought.

C   Horses

Horses are adorable animals. They are very strong and have been relied upon to support people throughout history. They have been important in farming, policing, and even warfare, but perhaps most often in sport. You can visit a racecourse to watch horses that have been taught to respond to commands racing in front of an enormous audience. People often place bets on which horse will win (if they can afford it). I would have more fun riding a horse along the seashore, or riding one to go walking in the forest. I can't think of anything more awesome than exploring the world on four legs!

Am I doing something wrong?

 Making a diphthong by trying to pronounce the other letter in the spelling.

✔ Ignore the spelling, and don't allow the articulators to move on this vowel sound. Record yourself making an /ɔ:/ and play it back. Is the vowel a smooth single sound, or is there a slight change?

It is common for this sound to be swapped specifically with the diphthong /əʊ/, as in GOAT. Refer to /əʊ/ (see page 81) and then compare the words below:

| goat–thought | goat–thought | goat–thought |
| boat–taught | boat–taught | boat–taught |

 Making the same vowel sound in the words THOUGHT and LOT.

✔ The /ɔ:/ vowel is long with lips very rounded, whilst the /ɒ/ vowel is short, with less rounded lips.

Watch the DVD to see and hear the difference between /ɔ:/ and /ɒ/.

First, check your lip position for both vowels using the *Vowel positioning diagram* (page 53). Ensure you have a clear lip shape change. Feel the tongue raise and lower slightly.

Now try these exercises:

130

1   Using a mirror, alternate between the two sounds:

awwww–o–awwww–o–awwww–o–awwww–o–awwww–o

ɔ: ɒ   ɔ: ɒ   ɔ: ɒ   ɔ: ɒ   ɔ: ɒ

2   Now try swapping between some words which have the sounds, like THOUGHT and LOT or:

| bought–hot | bought–hot | bought–hot |
| flaw–got | flaw–got | flaw–got |

3   The following sentence contains both /ɔ:/ vowel sounds (in CAPITALS) and /ɒ/ vowel sounds (in *italics*). Say the sentence, and compare the two.

T*o*m thOUght his h*o*t t*o*ffee sAUce and ch*o*colate shORtbread were Awesome, and n*o*t at All nAUghty.

 Rounding the lips too much and making a very tight vowel sound.

✔ Look in a mirror and ensure you are making the appropriate shape. Use the photo on page 76, and watch the DVD again.

Diphthongs in RP

The vowel sounds covered in units 19–30 were all monophthongs – single sounds. The group of vowel sounds we're going to look at now are diphthongs – vowels that are made up of two different sounds. To pronounce a diphthong correctly, you must see and feel the articulators move from the first sound to the second sound. The starting position of the sound is different to the final position.

For example, let's look at the word 'noon'. The lips and tongue are in the same position for the whole of the /uː/ monophthong: the *oo* part. Now let's compare that with the word 'noun'. There are two distinct vowel sounds in this word, and the articulators move from an open sound to a lip-rounded sound.

Remember: we are not introducing entirely new sounds – we are just combining existing ones. You already know how to make each individual vowel sound (from Units 19–30); all you have to learn now is how to put them together. So refer back to the monophthongs section whenever you need to. The relevant monophthongs are referenced in each unit.

Combining two sounds

In a diphthong, the first sound is always stronger than the second. Because of this, it can be tempting to shorten the sound by leaving the weaker, second sound out, or by making just one sound that is somewhere between the two. This often feels more fluent to learners but it is important that these vowels *always contain a movement*, however small.

To start, it is often easier to think of them as two separate sounds as this will ensure you make both. But remember, a diphthong is technically considered to be one sound, so each component sound should slide smoothly from one to another. In natural speech, there should be no break between the two.

Spelling

One of the big problems for learners is that the spelling of diphthongs can be very confusing and there are very few rules to help. Try and memorize a few words with different spellings for each diphthong. As before, we've listed the common spellings in each diphthong unit.

Am I doing something wrong?

In the diphthong units there are no *Am I doing something wrong?* sections. This is because the mistakes speakers make tend to be the same for all the diphthongs rather than different for each sound. Like the monophthongs, they also do not tend to change depending on your native language.

Instead, we have identified four main errors (A–D) which are general to most learners and have suggested exercises which help with each. You can apply these to any or all of the diphthongs wherever you feel you are struggling. Some of the exercises may seem a little laborious, especially if you have a high language level, but it is essential to make clear diphthongs if you are to be understood. Think of it as building the foundations of a house – if you don't get the foundations right, even the most beautiful house can fall down!

Error A

Many speakers turn diphthongs into a single sound (a monophthong).

1   Begin by reminding yourself how to make the two sounds of the diphthong (i.e. the two monophthongs).

2   Make sure that you have a mirror and the DVD in front of you.

3   Position your articulators for the first sound. This is Position 1. In the units we call it P1. Be clear and precise.

4   Position your articulators for the second sound, P2. Note the difference in position between the first and second sounds. Does the mouth start closed and finish open? Or vice versa?

5   Put the two sounds together. Start at P1 and move *slowly* to P2. Keep making sound throughout – the sound we make as we move from P1 to P2 is part of the diphthong. Repeat until you are confident you are making both P1 and P2 correctly.

6   The first part of the diphthong is always stronger, and the second part is weaker. Still looking in the mirror, try making the P1 long and loud, P2 quick and quiet.

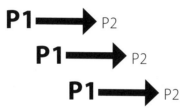

7   Finally, add some consonants either side to make sure you are maintaining a clear movement within words. You will naturally speed up when you are speaking full words and sentences, so the movement may feel smaller – but be sure it's still there. If it's not, repeat the steps above.

8   Record yourself and compare with the audio tracks in each unit.

Error B

Creating a dramatic shift between sounds rather than a smooth glide. This mistake is usually created by forgetting the sliding quality of the diphthong, and sharply breaking the vowel into its two component sounds.

1   Follow points 1 to 5 in error A (above). Make sure you are being precise with your two sounds.

2   Really focus on step 5 and check that you are making a gentle, gradual slide from the first position to the second.

3   Try saying some words that contain this sound, and check that they are remaining the same as when you practised them on their own. If not, then start again and slowly introduce consonants.

Error C

 Emphasizing the wrong half of the diphthong. This is a rhythmic issue. It may not seem like a big problem, but the importance of rhythm in English is huge and even the smallest rhythmic error can disrupt understanding. Remember, the first sound, P1, is always the strongest.

1 Start tapping your fingers in a STRONG–weak rhythm.

2 Repeat the words 'STRONG, weak, STRONG, weak, STRONG, weak', as you tap, to help you vocalize the rhythm.

3 Now change from the words to the sounds of the diphthong you are practising. Keep tapping!

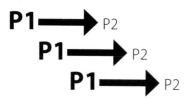

4 Check you have the rhythmic balance correct by recording and playing back.

5 Add in some consonants to make some words. You can still tap if it helps.

6 Habits can be hard to break, so if your balance shifts back, repeat the instructions above but use words with your diphthong all the way through.

Error D

 Using the wrong component sounds to make the diphthong.

1 Double check the component sounds of the diphthong by turning back to the relevant pages for each of the components.

2 Check that you are still pronouncing both of the component sounds accurately when you combine them together to make the diphthong.

3 Double check that you are still using the right pronunciation, no matter how the word is spelt.

Remember that all or just some of these processes can be useful with all or some of the diphthongs. Refer back to these pages whenever you are having difficulty.

GOAT /əʊ/

DVD

Make the sound

P1 is /ə/ as in LETT**ER**

Remember, the first sound is strongest.

P2 is /ʊ/ as in F**OO**T

When do I use this sound?

131

Spelling	Examples
o	no, both, note, rope, explode, bolt, over
oa	coat, oak
ou	soul, shoulder
ow	know, bowl
ough	though

! This diphthong is often indicated in spelling through the use of the formula

o + consonant + silent *e*

For example, the word 'hop' is pronounced with an /ɒ/, as in LOT, but if the spelling is 'hope', the *e* means you need to use the /əʊ/ sound. It is important to distinguish between these two sounds – 'hop' and 'hope' sound very different.

Now try it!

Say each of these words and sentences aloud. Then compare your pronunciation with the model on tracks 132–133.

132–133

A c<u>o</u>de   h<u>o</u>me   <u>o</u>z<u>o</u>ne   b<u>oa</u>t   fl<u>oa</u>t   b<u>ou</u>lder   c<u>o</u>lder

     t<u>oe</u>   gl<u>ow</u>   d<u>ou</u>gh   m<u>oa</u>t   fl<u>ow</u>n   <u>o</u>nly   er<u>o</u>sion

B   **1**   The mould was growing all over the damp stones in the garden of her coastal home.

     2   It was snowing over the rolling hills close to Toby's home.

     3   Although summer was nearly over, Sophie was hoping her roses would keep growing.

M**OU**TH /æʊ/

You may usually see this diphthong written with an /aʊ/ symbol which is a more old-fashioned version of RP. *We* have chosen to use the starting position of /æ/ as in CAP as this sound is more modern.

Make the sound

DVD

P1 is /æ/ as in C**A**P

Remember, the first sound is strongest.

P2 is /ʊ/ as in F**OO**T

When do I use this sound?

134

Spelling	Examples
ou	loud, round, out
ow	cow, down, allow

Now try it!

Say each of these words and sentences aloud. Then compare your pronunciation with the model on tracks 135–136.

135–136

A   proud   house   mountain   noun   trousers   town

around   brown   frown   bounce   shout   doubt

B   **1**   He was allowed into the house once she found out about the huge bunch of flowers.

     2   The owl was hiding outside, round the back of the house.

     3   She browsed the bargain bin and found a book about clouds for a pound.

FACE /eɪ/

Make the sound

P1 is /e/ as in DR**E**SS

Remember, the first sound is strongest.

P2 is /ɪ/ as in K**I**T

When do I use this sound?

137

Spelling	Examples
a	ace, name, cage, hate
ay	play, stayed
ea	great
ai	faith, wait
ei	eight, reindeer
ey	they, grey

Now try it!

Say each of these words and sentences aloud. Then compare your pronunciation with the model on tracks 138–139.

138–139

A

h<u>ay</u>	Sund<u>ay</u>	sp<u>a</u>de	l<u>a</u>te	Sp<u>ai</u>n	c<u>a</u>ke	f<u>ai</u>thful
<u>a</u>ge	w<u>ai</u>ter	<u>ei</u>ghty	m<u>a</u>ne	l<u>a</u>zy	am<u>a</u>zing	str<u>ai</u>ght

B

1 The stay at the lake hotel involved some great nature walks and lazy days under grey April skies.

2 They stayed out playing in the garden till late, in spite of the summer rain.

3 They ate plates of bacon sandwiches, followed by cake with raisins and maple syrup pancakes.

PRICE

/ʌɪ/

We have chosen to use the more modern, centralized vowel of /ʌ/ as in CUP to start this diphthong, but you may also see words like PRICE written with the symbol /aɪ/ in a pronunciation dictionary.

▶ Make the sound

DVD

P1 is /ʌ/ as in CUP

Remember, the first sound is strongest.

P2 is /ɪ/ as in KIT

When do I use this sound?

140

Spelling	Examples
i	like, write, ice, arrive
y	try, my, sky, shy, why
uy	buy
ei	height
ai	aisle
ui	beguile
igh	sight

Now try it!

Say each of these words and sentences aloud. Then compare your pronunciation with the model on tracks 141–142.

141–142

A pint   island   Friday   arrived   fly   night   guy   sly

drive   guide   disguise   rhyme   style   quite   night   high

B **1** The bride tried not to cry as she walked up the aisle.

2 The island was so tiny you could cycle across it in five minutes.

3 The sign for the airport was so high they drove right by it and missed their flight by five minutes.

CHOICE /ɔɪ/

DVD

▶ Make the sound

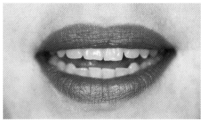

P1 is /ɔː/ as in THOUGHT

Remember, the first sound is strongest.

P2 is /ɪ/ as in KIT

When do I use this sound?

143

Spelling	Examples
oi	coin, noise, voice
oy	soya, toy, annoying

Now try it!

Say each of these words and sentences aloud. Then compare your pronunciation with the model on tracks 144–145.

144–145

A

poison	rejoice	moisture	boy	employer	choice
coy	oyster	buoy	joy	loiter	alloy

B

1   She was getting very annoyed by the noise the boys were making with their toys.

2   She enjoyed working near such a great choice of shops.

3   Her employer was impressed by how she toiled over her job.

NEAR

/ɪə/

DVD

Make the sound

P1 is /ɪ/ as in KIT

Remember, the first sound is strongest.

P2 is /ə/ as in LETTER

When do I use this sound?

146

Spelling	Examples
e	here, hero
ee	beer, career
ea	ear, fear
ie	pier, cashier
ei	weird

Now try it!

Say each of these words and sentences aloud. Then compare your pronunciation with the model on tracks 147–148.

147–148

A really   appeared   idea   mysterious   period   spear

cheer   meerkat   serious   theatre   superior   clear

B 1 Maria pierced Sophia's ears.

2 The mysterious fear of the eerie pier brought her to tears.

3 It's hard to find a good Madeira cake here in Korea.

HAIR

/eə/

This diphthong is always spelt with an *r*, like the /ɜː/ of NURSE. Look at *The spoken and the silent* r (page 50) for how and when to pronounce the *r*.

 Make the sound

DVD

P1 is /e/ as in DR**E**SS

Remember, the first sound is strongest.

P2 is /ə/ as in LETT**ER**

When do I use this sound?

149

Spelling	Examples
ear	bear
ar	share
air	fair
ay	mayor
ere	there
eir	their

Now try it!

Say each of these words and sentences aloud. Then compare your pronunciation with the model on tracks 150–151.

150–151

A p<u>ear</u>   w<u>ear</u>   sw<u>ear</u>ing   p<u>air</u>ing   f<u>air</u>y   d<u>air</u>y   v<u>ary</u>

st<u>ar</u>ing   b<u>are</u>   p<u>rayer</u>   c<u>ar</u>ing   comp<u>are</u>   prec<u>ar</u>ious   fl<u>air</u>

B **1**   See that town square over there? There's a great hairdresser just by the stairs.

2   This area is known for its dairy fare.

3   Mary has various pairs of shoes, and still she swears she has nothing to wear!

CURE

/ʊə/

Make the sound

DVD

P1 is /ʊ/ as in F**OO**T

Remember, the first sound is strongest.

P2 is /ə/ as in LETT**ER**

When do I use this sound?

152

Spelling	Examples
ur	pure, mature, tour
oor	poor, moor

Now try it!

Say each of these words and sentences aloud. Then compare your pronunciation with the model on tracks 153–154.

153–154

A s<u>ur</u>e   p<u>ur</u>ely   sec<u>ur</u>e   f<u>ur</u>ious   obsc<u>ur</u>e

m<u>oor</u>   t<u>our</u>ing   mat<u>ur</u>e   d<u>ur</u>ing   c<u>ur</u>e

B **1** Those poor people having to go on a tour of the moor in this weather.

2 Muriel was furious about the lapse in her personal security.

3 She was curious about the maturity of the teenage security guard.

Evolving sound

This is an evolving sound in RP. In the past, any words in our spelling examples above were pronunced with the /ʊə/ diphthong. But recently standard speech has shifted and some of the words have merged with the /ɔː/ monophthong, as in 'thought'. It is happening at different times with different words, but as an example, the word 'poor' which has been traditionally pronounced with an /ʊə/, is now frequently heard with an /ɔː/ in RP speech. Both sounds are fine, but the THOUGHT vowel is more modern. Please listen to both versions on audio tracks 152 and 155.

155

p<u>ure</u>, mat<u>ur</u>e, t<u>our</u>, p<u>oor</u>, m<u>oor</u>

Connecting your speech

Connecting your speech

So far, we have mainly focused on individual sounds in isolation. But when you are speaking, words start to join up with one another, and some interesting things can happen at word boundaries – where one word meets another.

We have seen this in Unit 4 with the *Assimilation in nasal sounds* (see page 22) and also in Unit 18 with *The spoken and silent* r (see page 50). It is the same with other letters at different word boundaries. Sometimes the pronunciation of the written letter disappears, sometimes it changes and sometimes a new sound is added to help link the two sounds.

Why do we do this?

It may sound complicated, but these are not extra rules with no purpose. In each case, they are part of the process of making the mouth move from one shape to another. These changes happen when it's simply easier to miss a sound out, or to add or change one to make the connected phrase feel more natural.

If you don't do it, it is not always wrong, but it will slow you down and might make you sound very deliberate – as if you are making a very special point. In order to sound natural, you want to make your connected speech flow, and the examples in Units 39–41 will help you to achieve this.

In Unit 39, *Changing sounds*, we will look at where the sounds change or are pronounced differently depending on the context. In Unit 40, *Linking sounds*, we will look at where new sounds intrude or are added in to make connected speech easier. In Unit 41, we will look at where some words are run together and some vowel sounds are missed out entirely.

39

Changing sounds

1 Two different pronunciations of *the*

156

The word 'the' has two different pronunciations depending on whether the following word begins with a vowel sound or a consonant sound.

Before a vowel sound, the word 'the' is pronounced with a long vowel sound, /iː/ as in SHEEP:

/ðiː/

   the apple   the orange

Before a consonant sound, 'the' is pronounced with a schwa:

/ðə/

   the grapes   the banana

Listeners would be expecting to hear the unstressed sound before the consonant. If you used the long vowel sound instead, they may think that there was something very special about the grapes or the banana.

But remember, it's all about the *sound* that the next word begins with, not the spelling:

| the hour | /ðiː æʊə/ |
| the unit | /ðə juːnɪt/ |

2 Unreleased consonants

We learnt about plosive consonants in Units 1, 2 and 3. The plosive consonants are /t/, /d/, /p/, /b/, /k/, /g/. They usually involve the blocking and releasing of the airflow. But, when a plosive consonant is the last sound in a phrase, or if it is followed by another consonant sound, it is often *unreleased*. This means that you set your mouth up ready to make the sound, and block the air, but then do not release the air.

Listen to the audio tracks for these units to remind yourself what these look and sound like.

Now try it!

157

should think	Yes, well I should think so too.
sit	There's nowhere for us to sit.
stop looking	Stop looking at me like that.
club member	He's a loyal club member.
quick change	I need to make a quick change.
big challenge	The job is a really big challenge.

If you do release the sound, it will give the impression that you are being formal, or very careful. These sounds wouldn't usually be released in rapid connected speech.

3 Consonant–vowel

If a word that ends with a consonant sound (e.g. 'test', 'drop') is followed by a word that starts with a vowel sound ('test us', 'drop in'), you must fully pronounce the consonant on the end of the word, and use it to join onto the next vowel.

Now try it!

Listen and compare the difference between a consonant–vowel combination and a consonant–consonant combination.

got⌣another	He's got⌣another girlfriend.
got promoted	And he got promoted.
could⌣ask	You could⌣ask for help with this.
could fix	Or I could fix it myself.
drop⌣everything	Drop⌣everything and come over!
drop round	Sorry, I can't drop round today.
add⌣up	The small costs really add⌣up.
add to	They really add to our money problems.
back⌣on	We got back⌣on Tuesday afternoon.
back Wednesday	I thought you were back Wednesday.

If you don't join the two words together, your speech will sound too jumpy.

4 Twin consonants

When a word ends with a consonant, and the same consonant starts the next word, like 'don't talk' or 'stop pulling', we only say the sound once. We use it to link the two words.

You will feel a light pressure hold at the end of the first word, which you don't release until the start of the second word. If you are saying it right, it is impossible to tell where one sound ends and another begins.

Now try it!

Try linking these phrases ...

don't⌣tell	Don't⌣tell me you didn't know.
could⌣do	We could⌣do that if you like.
stop⌣putting	Stop⌣putting your food on my shelf.
grab⌣both	Could you grab⌣both of them?
big⌣game	There's a big⌣game on tonight.
make⌣copies	Could you make⌣copies of these?
this⌣song	I love this⌣song!

... then, listen and compare.

Linking sounds

1 The linking /j/

When a word ends with the vowel sounds of PRICE (/ʌɪ/), FACE (/eɪ/), CHOICE (/ɔɪ/), or SHEEP (/iː/), and it is followed by a word that starts with a vowel, they are usually linked by a small /j/ sound as in YES.

Now try it!

160

Try inserting the /j/ sound into these phrases, then listen and compare.

I/ʲ/always have.   Coy,/ʲ/aren't you!

They/ʲ/avoided it.   He/ʲ/absolutely can.

2 The linking /w/

When a word ends with the sound of GOOSE (/uː/), GOAT (/əʊ/), and MOUTH (/æʊ/), and is followed by a word that starts with a vowel, they are usually linked by a small /w/ sound, as in WEEK. This is because all these vowels are made with rounded lips, and as the lips move back, they make a /w/ sound. All these vowels are made with rounded lips, and as the lips move back from this shape they make a /w/ sound.

Now try it!

161

Try inserting the /w/ sound into these phrases, then listen and compare.

You/ʷ/only asked.   How/ʷ/are you?

Go/ʷ/away!

3 t or d becomes /tʃ/ or /dʒ/

When a word ends with a t or d and the following word starts with a y, when speaking quickly you will hear a /tʃ/ sound as in 'choke', or a /dʒ/ sound as in 'joke'. If you slow down a little, it is possible to make the sounds separately. In RP, it doesn't matter whether you keep the sounds separate or run them together, but you should be able to recognize both.

Now try it!

162

Listen first to the sentences with the /t/ or /d/ and a separate /j/ pronunciation.

Don't you remember what we said?   But you always said it would be easy.

Why can't you give me an answer?   What was the meal we had yesterday?

Hurry up and put your shoes on.   You should use whichever you prefer.

163

Now listen to the same sentences with the /tʃ/ or /dʒ/ pronunciation. Repeat both versions. Which one feels most comfortable for you? It won't really matter which one you use, but /t/, /d/ + /j/ is a little more formal.

Contractions

Some very common words in English are run together to form a new word. This is called a contraction and when it happens, some vowel sounds get missed out entirely. In spoken English, it's not the exception – it is the norm; and it's important to use these contractions, otherwise you will sound too formal even in very formal settings!

In written English the missing letter is identified by an apostrophe. There's one in this sentence. Can you identify the missing letter and sound?

It was the /ɪ/ sound of 'is' in the contraction 'there's'. The sound is completely excluded, but people often hear it as a schwa or try to pronounce the /ɪ/ sound.

Contraction happens so often in spoken English that it is difficult to give a complete list. Here are some of the main ones. Listen to the audio carefully to hear the difference between the long form and the contraction.

164

Long form		Contraction	Long form		Contraction
what is	→	what's	they will	→	they'll
he is	→	he's	it will	→	it'll
that is	→	that's	we have	→	we've
I am	→	I'm	where have	→	where've
can not	→	can't	I have	→	I've
do not	→	don't	I would	→	I'd
would not	→	wouldn't	they would	→	they'd
will not	→	won't	she had	→	she'd
you are	→	you're	you had	→	you'd
they are	→	they're			

165

Now try it!

Listen to the recording, and try to hear all the stress patterns created by contractions. Then repeat the sentences, making sure that you use those patterns yourself.

1 <u>Isn't</u> it a lovely day! <u>I'm</u> going to go for a walk.

2 <u>What's</u> his name again? <u>I'm</u> sorry, <u>I've</u> forgotten!

3 <u>I'd</u> love to try a sip of your drink. <u>Don't</u> worry, I <u>won't</u> drink it all!

4 <u>Where've</u> you been all this time? <u>We've</u> been waiting for hours.

5 <u>Don't</u> take on so much responsibility if <u>it'll</u> make you feel stressed.

6 I <u>can't</u> believe you <u>didn't</u> tell me <u>you're</u> going to have a baby!

7 <u>That's</u> all <u>I've</u> had time to prepare. Sorry, I thought <u>I'd</u> have longer.

8 I <u>don't</u> know whether <u>they'll</u> stay for dinner.

9 <u>What's</u> the point of getting angry? <u>He'll</u> never change.

10 <u>You're</u> such a great person – I'm so pleased <u>we've</u> met.

Section D

RP rhythm

Finding the rhythm of RP

Have you noticed how every language has its own distinct rhythm? You don't even need to be able to understand a language to recognize its tunes and patterns. Hearing the rhythm of a language will help you to understand its character. This character is created by the shape of the language, which in turn has an effect on the speaker's anatomy and breathing patterns.

Changing the rhythm you use to communicate will mean changing how quickly or slowly you speak; this will then mean adapting your breathing and maybe even your thinking. It can feel strange at first but it will soon begin to feel more natural.

Finding the rhythm of RP might make you feel louder or softer, faster or slower, more emphatic or less powerful. You might associate this way of communicating with being in a particular mood because it isn't your usual way of speaking; but to a native English speaker it's nothing unusual. Remember, feeling different is a good thing; it means you are breaking habits, softening your accent and finding the rhythm of RP.

Stress and intonation

When we talk about the rhythm of RP, we are referring to the musical way in which words and syllables combine in speech. Speech rhythm is created by a combination of stress patterns and intonation patterns.

Stress
Stress is the contrast between strong and weak syllables within words, or strong and weak words within sentences. These contrasts are created through vowel reduction, by using 'the schwa', the /ə/ sound you learnt about in Unit 19.

Intonation
Intonation is the tune of your speech – the combination of different notes used in a sentence.

These two elements work together to create the rhythm of RP. They can't be separated; you need one to make the other. So although parts of this *RP Rhythm* section deal with stress and other parts with intonation, you will always be working on both.

What you will learn

In the following 11 units, you will learn:
- why stress and intonation are so important
- how intonation works and what it means when you use it
- how stress works and what difference it makes to meaning
- the importance of the schwa in English rhythm.

42

It's not what you say, but the way that you say it

Stress and intonation are incredibly important in English. They add to meaning just as much as your choice of words. You can pronounce every syllable in a sentence perfectly, but without the right stress or intonation you will still be misunderstood.

Surprised? Let's explore how stress or intonation can affect understanding. Look at these pictures:

'I can't believe you did this!'   'I can't believe you did this!'

The pictures demonstrate that it is possible to use the same sentence in two different situations and for it to mean completely different things, depending on how it is stressed.

Now try it!

166

How would you say the sentence above differently so that it makes sense for each picture?

Listen and compare what *you* said to the voice on track 166.

Using stress to make your point

In anything you say, the important words need to stand out. There are three ways you can do this:

1   Make a sound or word last longer.

2   Say a sound or word louder.

3   Say a sound or word in a different pitch.

The most important thing about stress is that you use it to make your point – whatever that point may be. You can choose to stress almost any word but when you do, everything around it will become less important (shorter, quieter, more monotone).

You can hear this in the examples below. Notice how the meaning of the same sentence changes as a different word is stressed each time.

1 On Saturday morning, she turns twenty.	*And not before!*
2 On Saturday morning, she turns twenty.	*Not Friday, not Sunday, but Saturday.*
3 On Saturday morning, she turns twenty.	*Not the afternoon or evening.*
4 On Saturday morning, she turns twenty.	*That girl over there.*
5 On Saturday morning, she turns twenty.	*She isn't twenty yet.*
6 On Saturday morning, she turns twenty.	*Not twenty-one.* or *Can you believe it?*

Now try it!

Say these sentences. Stress the right word to change the meaning of what you are saying.

1 I had salad for dinner on Tuesday.	*Not Wednesday.*
2 I had salad for dinner on Tuesday.	*Not for lunch.*
3 I had salad for dinner on Tuesday.	*Not pizza.*
4 I had salad for dinner on Tuesday.	*You didn't, though.*

Now listen to check whether you were right.

The roller coaster of English speech

Pitch

In RP, we very often use **pitch** to stress an important word in a sentence. Pitch is the note that we speak on, and we can use either a higher or a lower note. When you are listening to someone speaking in English, these high- and low-pitched words will help you identify the words you need to pay attention to.

The rise and fall of the pitch is called intonation. When you first use it, you might feel it is exaggerated. But it isn't! For the listener, it is normal and completely necessary. Intonation is not additional to the accent, or a finishing touch – it is an essential ingredient in fluent communication.

Now try it!

Listen to these sentences – can you hear which words are spoken on the highest or lowest notes? These will be the most important to understanding what is being said. Put an ↑ arrow over the word if it's spoken on the highest note, or a ↓ over the word, if it's spoken on the lowest note.

1. He was so gorgeous!
2. She was being ridiculous.
3. It was a really hard exam.
4. He was wearing such hideous shoes.
5. I'm too tired for this.
6. I'll only be a few minutes.

 Check your answers in the answer key on page 146.

How do I do it?

Hearing the intonation is the first stage in being able to reproduce it. So now that you've made a start, let's try another exercise.

Intonation and meaning are hard to separate, but to begin with, we are going to ask you to *forget the words* and just listen for pitch. The steps below will help you to do that.

Now try it!

Step 1

- On track 170 is a weather report. (See the box on the facing page for the full text.) Listen to the track but *don't* listen to the words – listen to the pitch instead.
- Follow the pitch by moving your hand up and down with the speaker's voice.
- How much does the pitch move – a little or a lot? Move your hand higher or lower to reflect that.

By matching the words with movement in your hand, you will start to understand how your voice has to move when you are speaking.

DVD

Watch Step 1 on the DVD to see exactly what you should be doing.

Step 2

- Now listen again and start to match your voice to the movement of your hand.
- At first, don't use the words. Just let your voice move with the different pitches that you hear. Use an 'mmmmm' sound.

In Step 2 you are *singing* the passage. Don't worry, no one can hear you! You can hear us doing this in audio track 170.

Step 3

- Now that you understand the melody of the passage, listen again to how this fits with the words, and try to put it all together, this time saying the words.
- Record yourself and see if you have captured the same melody as you heard on the audio track.

This is Jane Andrews with your local weather report. Well, we really couldn't ask for a more perfect start to spring. At the moment it's fifteen degrees in Trafalgar Square and there isn't a cloud in sight. The great news is that we're expecting the blue skies and sunshine to last for the rest of the day. The not-so-great news is that although there is currently only a ten per cent chance of showers today, this good weather won't be lasting for long. It's raining cats and dogs up north, and that weather front will be moving south overnight and covering the whole of the South East by 7 a.m., so don't forget your umbrella in the morning! That's all from me for now, stay tuned for your local news.

Low, lowest, high, highest

Now let's explore just how much possibility for pitch range you have in your voice!

- First, say the word 'me' on a note that feels comfortable for you.
- Now pick a note that is a little higher ... say 'higher'.
- Then a note that is higher still ... say 'highest'. And repeat.

🎧
171

me–higher–highest–me–higher–highest

- Now come back to 'me'.
- Then pick a note that is a little lower ... say 'lower'.
- Now pick a note that is lower still ... say 'lowest'.

me–lower–lowest–me–lower–lowest

- Now try a few combinations of these notes:

me–lower–higher–me–highest–lower–higher–lowest–
me–highest–higher–lowest–me

Now you have found your range, you are ready to put it into action.

44

Intonation in action

Intonation patterns provide extra information to the listener. Without this extra information, a listener will find it very hard to understand what you really mean. The words you use tell your listener what you are saying, but intonation shows how you feel about saying it. It is *emotional* punctuation.

172

Listen to three simple conversations. The words are the same but the meaning is very different.

1   - How are you?

- Fine. [*But I'm also really annoyed with you.*]

2   - How are you?

- Fine. [*I'm in a great mood!*]

3   - How are you?

- Fine. [*I'm not really fine at all – I'm actually feeling very sad.*]

Now try it!

1   Look at the following conversation:

- Would you mind helping me with the washing up?

- Yes, okay.

Give the response 'Yes, okay', but make it mean three completely different things. Just say 'Yes, okay'.

1   Yes, okay.   *(I'd be happy to help.)*

2   Yes, okay.   *(I'd really rather not, it's boring, but I suppose I should.)*

3   Yes, okay.   *(Anything to stop your constant nagging.)*

173

How do your answers compare with the ones on the recording? Monitor your pitch using hand gestures like you did in the previous unit. Does your intonation pattern match the one on the recording? If not, do you need to lower or raise your pitch at a certain point?

2   Try another one:

- Are you sure you locked the door?

- Yes.

1   Yes.   *(Absolutely, definitely.)*

2   Yes.   *(I think I did, but now you ask, I'm not sure.)*

3   Yes.   *(Why do you keep asking? For the hundredth time, yes I locked the door.)*

174

Listen and compare your responses.

You are starting to understand the importance of intonation when speaking English. Subtle differences in pitch can make the difference between being really understood, and people hearing the words but still completely missing the point of what you are saying.

45

A rising tone

We've learnt that intonation is all about the high and low notes used to emphasize and make longer the important words in a phrase, and to diminish and move quickly over the unimportant ones. And we've learnt also that there is a range from lowest to highest which we can use. But what about the pattern of those notes, and how do we know whether to use the higher or the lower ones when we speak?

Let's learn some new words before we go on. If the pitch ends up higher than it started, we call it a *rising tone* ➚ , and if the pitch ends up lower than it started, we call it a *falling tone* ➘ .

Two types of rising tone

Pitch can rise directly ➚ – this is called a *direct rise*, or indirectly ↰ – this is called a *fall–rise*.

Both of these tones indicate that there is more to be said, that you haven't finished speaking. But they do it in different ways:

➚ A direct rise means you are curious, you agree, you are excited, or you are surprised.

↰ The fall–rise means doubt, uncertainty, disbelief.

Now try it!

175

Use the Steps 1 and 2 from Unit 43 to make the shape, and *sing* the different tones.

1 a direct rising tone

2 a fall–rising tone

3 contrasting direct rising and fall–rising tones. Notice the differences between the two.

How far should I go?

The amount that pitch rises also changes the meaning of what you are saying. Generally, the more dramatic the pitch movement the stronger the emotional drive behind what you are saying. You will hear this in action in the sentences below.

Now try it!

These are the most common examples of when you would use a directly rising or fall–rising tone. Listen to the examples, and practise them yourself.

176

1 Making a list (excluding the last item):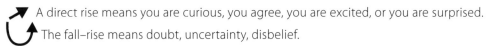

We need to buy apples, sugar, oats, honey, rhubarb...

I like his hair, his smile, his aftershave…

The recipe says six carrots, four leeks…

2   Sympathy:

Oh, you poor thing.

I'm sure she didn't mean to hurt your feelings!

Aw, you look so tired!

3   Indicating doubt:

I suppose he meant well.

I will if I have to…

Do you really think purple suits your skin tone…?

4   Asking a question with a yes/no answer:

Are you hungry?

Is there time for tea?

Are you a size 12?

5   Challenging someone:

Is that the normal process?

Are you the only manager?

Are you sure?

6   Starting a conversation:

Can I help you with something?

Are you lost?

Welcome to the school.

46

A falling tone

Two types of falling tone

Falling tones can also move directly, called a *direct fall* 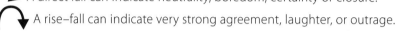, or indirectly, a *rise–fall* .
Both tones signal the end of a topic or conversation, and suggest that there is nothing more
to be said, but again, they do so in different ways.

A direct fall can indicate neutrality, boredom, certainty or closure.

A rise–fall can indicate very strong agreement, laughter, or outrage.

Now try it!

Use the steps 1 and 2 from Unit 43 to make the shape, and *sing* the different tones.

1 a direct falling tone

2 a rise–falling tone

3 contrasting direct falling, and rise–falling tones. Notice the differences between the
two.

How far should I go?

As before, the amount that you change your pitch changes the meaning of what you are
saying. Generally the more dramatic the pitch movement, the stronger the emotion behind
what you are saying. You will hear this in action in the sentences below.

Now try it!

These are the most common examples of when you would use a falling or rise–falling tone.
Listen to the examples, and practise yourself.

1 Finality:

> The divorce came through on Friday.
>
> Then I guess there's nothing more to say.
>
> Aha, there is it. We found it.

2 Certainty:

> The red dress is nicer.
>
> He's a really good person.
>
> It's a great time of year for asparagus.

3 Boredom:

> For the seventeenth time, no, you don't look fat.
>
> This journey's taking forever.
>
> This book is so dull, and the exercises are tedious.

4 Complaining:

Life is so unfair.

Why can't you come to my party?

I'm always the last to know.

5 Outrage:

No! Of course I didn't steal it!

I only use organic veg in my cooking!

How dare you!

6 Flirting:

Oh stop it! You're being so naughty!

I'm sure I'd remember your face.

I think you should ask me out.

! Remember that intonation is subjective. You can stress anything you say, however you like, but don't be tempted to apply the same pattern in everything you say – a rigid tune is as bad as no tune at all. The rules outlined here and in Unit 45 are just some guidelines and examples for how intonation can be interpreted.

47

Why is stress so important?

English rhythm isn't just about intonation – it's also about stress. So everything you've learnt about intonation relies on also using stress appropriately.

English is all about balance. In order to make the important words really stand out, you have to make the unimportant words and syllables almost disappear. If you don't get this balance right, you will sound over-emphatic as you'll be stressing everything. In order to find this balance you will need to learn the most common sound in the English language; **the schwa**.

To understand when to use the schwa, you will first need to understand syllables – and learn to hear them clearly.

Hearing the syllables

Syllables are the small units of speech containing a vowel sound. Words always have at least one syllable, but often more. Each one is like a beat of music

Let's take the word 'car'. This word has one syllable – one vowel sound /k<u>ɑː</u>/. Clap each time you say a syllable:

179

| car | car | car | car | car |

/kɑː/   /kɑː/   /kɑː/   /kɑː/   /kɑː/

Now, take the word 'carrot'. This word has two syllables – two vowel sounds /k<u>æ</u>/ and /ɹ<u>ət</u>/. Clap each time you say a syllable:

car-rot   car-rot   car-rot   car-rot   car-rot

/kæ-ɹət/   /kæ-ɹət/   /kæ-ɹət/   /kæ-ɹət/   /kæ-ɹət/

Now, lets take the word 'character'. This word has three syllables – three vowel sounds /k<u>æ</u>-ɹ<u>ə</u>k-t<u>ə</u>/. Clap each time you say a syllable:

cha-rac-ter   cha-rac-ter   cha-rac-ter   cha-rac-ter   cha-rac-ter

/kæ-ɹək-tə/   /kæ-ɹək-tə/   /kæ-ɹək-tə/   /kæ-ɹək-tə/   /kæ-ɹək-tə/

Now try it!

Try clapping the right number of syllables for the following words. (Remember, some words have silent letters that might make them look like they contain more beats.)

1

one-syllable words	cat, mug, one, shoe, scarf, thought, note, bag, hand
two-syllable words	happy, very, because, parrot, business, paper
three-syllable words	potato, computer, fantastic, studio, telephone
four-syllable words	unusual, competitive, television, particular
five-syllable words	participation, enthusiastic, characteristic, imagination

180

2   Listen to these words. They all have a different number of syllables. Put them in order from the least syllables to the most.

unhappiness   ghost   organize   pronunciation   waiter

How many syllables does each word have?

   Check your answers in the answer key on page 146.

Sounds, not spelling

Don't be distracted by the spelling. You know that many words have silent letters, and that two vowels written together are often just one sound.

Now try it!

181

1   Here are some more words. Listen to them and write them in the correct column.

paper	house	reality	fantastic	big
syllable	language	undeniable	authority	increase
argument	truth	prominent	indiscriminate	parking
observation	weaker	education	monosyllabic	through

one syllable	two syllables	three syllables	four syllables	five syllables

   Check your answers in the answer key on page 146.

182

2   Let's try another exercise to see if you can hear the odd one out. You're going to hear four words for each question. Which one has a different number of syllables (more or less) than the others in the group? Write the word and why it is different from the others. The first one is done for you.

   1   business – has two syllables and the others have three

   2

   3

   4

   5

   6

   Check your answers in the answer key on page 146.

In any word that has more than one syllable, one syllable will be the most prominent, and this means the other syllables will become weaker. As we said at the start of this unit, we make syllables weaker by replacing the vowel with a **schwa**. Hopefully, you will have noticed some of those schwas in the audio tracks in this unit.

We'll learn more about listening for and making the schwa sound in the next unit.

48

The schwa

The schwa – often called the neutral vowel – is the unstressed or weak vowel sound that we use in RP to contrast with the stressed sounds.

Listen to audio track 77, from Unit 19, to remind yourself of what a schwa should sound like.

What are the spelling rules?

When you hear the schwa in a word, you can't tell what vowel letter (*a, e, i, o,* or *u*) it was spelt with. The sound can be represented by any 'regular' vowel, regardless of spelling, in a syllable that isn't stressed (although a letter 'i' on its own is less likely to become a schwa).

Listen to these two-syllable words. The unstressed vowel, underlined here, is the schwa. Notice how it is a very dull, uninteresting sound without much character of its own.

a   <u>a</u>bout

e   bett<u>e</u>r

i   penc<u>i</u>l

o   t<u>o</u>day

u   s<u>u</u>pport

Now try it!

These two-syllable words above contain beats, but now we hear that one is stronger than the other. Listen again and clap the beats of the words that you hear just as you did in the previous unit but this time make one louder and stronger, and the other quieter and softer.

clap-**clap**   or   **clap**-clap

You may have never heard of the schwa, but it is the most common vowel sound in English and the most important sound for you to learn. If vowels were people at a party, the schwa would be the waiter who keeps re-filling your glass without you even noticing. It's not interesting, it doesn't stand out, but without it things wouldn't run smoothly. When you're using the schwa correctly, you will hardly be aware of it, but you'll be using it all the time!

Hearing the schwa in context

Let's contrast the neutral – sounding schwa with some other, stronger vowel shapes.

Let's start with the /uː/ sound, as in GOOSE. You can remind yourself of this vowel on page 70.

- Look in the mirror: when you're making the /uː/ sound as in GOOSE, your lips should be strongly rounded and you should feel the back of your tongue lifting high in the back of your mouth. It is a long vowel sound.

- When you're making the schwa /ə/, you should see your lips relax, and become neutral. Your tongue should be flat and soft in your mouth. It is a short vowel sound.

Try this exercise, using the video clip for guidance:

DVD

uː ə   uː ə   uː ə   uː ə   uː ə

Now let's try comparing the schwa with the /iː/ sound as in SHEEP. You can remind yourself of this vowel on page 60.

- Look in a mirror: when you're making the SHEEP vowel, your lips should be very slightly spread, and you should feel the front of your tongue lifting high in the front of your mouth.

- When you're making the schwa, you should see your lips relax and become neutral. Your tongue should be flat and soft in your mouth.

Try this exercise, using the video clip for guidance:

DVD

iː ə   iː ə   iː ə   iː ə   iː ə

Now try it!

184

1 Let's try spotting the schwa sound in some actual words. Listen and underline the vowel letter or letters that are represented by a schwa.

China   surprise   forget   visa   station
focus   special   object   regard   beside

  Check your answers in the answer key on page 146.

English is a stress-timed language

Most languages are either syllable-timed or stress-timed. In a syllable-timed language every syllable takes up roughly the same amount of time. In a stress-timed language, some syllables are longer and more prominent than others. Here is an example of the same sentence, spoken with syllable timing, and then stress timing. Look and listen to the two different rhythms of the sentence below.

185

He can have as many sandwiches as he likes, but it mustn't cost more than seven pounds fifty.

English is a stress-timed language. This means that when you speak, the important syllables or words need to be made more obvious than the unimportant ones for what you are saying to make sense. Remember, stress is relative, so to make something bigger we have to make other things smaller. In English, we could represent the sentence above like this:

He can have as many sandwiches as he likes, but it mustn't cost more than seven pounds fifty.

Even the Queen uses the schwa

Many learners believe that to sound clear you need to pronounce each syllable clearly. When people are taught English they are often told that speaking 'correctly' means pronouncing every vowel distinctly. So it can feel strange to reduce these clear sounds to the neutral schwa. But it is really important that you use the schwa, otherwise your speech will sound fake – even the Queen uses the schwa! In reality, you will sound far more like a native speaker and be more easily understood by using it.

49

Word stress

As we learned in the previous unit, any word with two or more syllables will have a stressed syllable and an unstressed syllable. But the pattern is not regular. For example, in the word 'listen', you stress the first syllable – /ˈlɪsən/. But in the word 'forgot', you stress the second syllable – /fəˈgɒt/.

How do you know which syllable to stress?

Unfortunately, the rules of stress pronunciation are quite difficult. You will have to learn many individual words on their own. When you hear a new word being used for the first time:

- listen and repeat
- check in a pronunciation dictionary where the stress is marked with a ' just before the stressed syllable, like this /fəˈgɒt/ and /ˈlɪsən/.

If in doubt, ask a native speaker stressing the syllables, 'Is it <u>for</u>got or for<u>got</u>?'

However, there are a few rules to make the learning process a little simpler. For example, if you see a word with con- at the start, like 'container', the con- syllable will usually not be stressed.

Now try it!

186

1   In the table below are some useful prefixes that are usually pronounced with a schwa. Listen to the words and complete the table.

about	~~container~~	~~believe~~	forgive	~~computer~~	~~decide~~
prepare	~~today~~	respect	~~pronounce~~	~~occur~~	complain
demand	~~forget~~	begin	forbid	condition	again
tomorrow	~~report~~	occasion	because	~~allow~~	provide
convince	support	delicious	regret	~~predict~~	~~supply~~
present (vb)	commit	surprise	tonight	observe	professional

a- allow	be-* believe	com- computer	con- container
_____ _____	_____ _____	_____ _____	_____ _____
de-* decide	for- forget	pre-* predict	pro- pronounce
_____ _____	_____ _____	_____ _____	_____ _____
re-* report	su- supply	to- today	o- occur
_____ _____	_____ _____	_____ _____	_____ _____

> * These prefixes can be pronounced with a weak /ɪ/ as in KIT, instead of a schwa. For a full explanation of the weak /ɪ/ rules, and where you can find them in words, turn to Appendix 1 on page 142. There you will also find an expanded table of examples of the schwa in word stress.

2 There are also a series of common suffixes that are pronounced with a schwa, such as *-ion* as in 'television'. Listen to the words and complete the table.

teacher	favour	~~India~~	panda	~~lawyer~~	~~government~~
anxious	curious	China	professor	director	complication
dollar	~~harbour~~	~~doctor~~	sugar	Dalston	photography
~~delicate~~	separate	~~England~~	~~biology~~	occasion	commitment
~~local~~	tribal	Boston	colour	Iceland	~~Birmingham~~
~~Oxford~~	~~democracy~~	Scotland	apology	leader	~~information~~
Watford	~~fabulous~~	Fulham	Stratford	Graham	~~Kensington~~
~~polar~~	intricate	privacy	accuracy	historical	excitement

-er	*-or*	*-our*	*-ar*
lawyer	doctor	harbour	polar
_____	_____	_____	_____
_____	_____	_____	_____
-a	*-ous*	*-ate*	*-logy/-graphy*
India	fabulous	delicate	biology
_____	_____	_____	_____
_____	_____	_____	_____
-ion	*-acy*	*-ment*	*-al*
information	democracy	government	local
_____	_____	_____	_____
_____	_____	_____	_____
-ton	*-ford*	*-land*	*-ham*
Kensington	Oxford	England	Birmingham
_____	_____	_____	_____
_____	_____	_____	_____

You can check your answers to both of these exercises in the answer key on page 146.

113

50

Irregularities in word stress

Let's look at some irregularities in stress patterns. Here are three rules to help you:

1 When a word can be a noun or a verb, the stress sometimes moves

Sometimes, we use the same word for a noun and a verb. But we very often stress them differently. Two-syllable nouns are usually stressed on the first syllable, but two-syllable verbs are usually stressed on the second syllable. Listen to these stress patterns.

188

noun	verb	noun	verb
record	to record	project	to project
refuse	to refuse	contest	to contest
second	to second	permit	to permit
research	to research	export	to export
present	to present	protest	to protest

Now try it!

Read these sentences aloud, concentrating on the syllable stress in each word from the table above:

1   What year did the Beatles *record* this *record*?

2   I *refuse* to pick up your *refuse* from the floor.

3   This is the *second* time your boss has been *seconded* to help with the audit.

4   I'd like you to *research* where we can find some more current *research* on the topic.

5   All members of the group were *present* when the information was *presented*.

6   It isn't possible to *project* how successful this *project* will be.

7   If you don't think it was a fair *contest*, you should *contest* the result.

8   I'm not sure if you're *permitted* to park here without a *permit*.

9   I'm going to *export* all these *exports* to my international sales teams.

10 We all went to the *protest* because we wanted to *protest* about the cuts.

189

Now listen and compare.

2 In compound words, the stress usually falls on the first word

A compound word is made when two smaller words are put together. Sometimes this creates a new single word, sometimes a hyphenated word and sometimes the two words remain separate on the page; but in all cases they combine to create a new meaning.

190

The stress in a compound structure usually falls on the first word in the pair.

Listen to these stress patterns.

<u>land</u>line   <u>car</u> park   <u>air</u>port   <u>class</u>room   <u>book</u> shelf   <u>hot</u>dog

But there are some exceptions to this rule when both parts of the compound structure get equal stress:

- if the first word in the compound is an adjective:

  <u>twin</u> <u>bed</u>   <u>cell</u> <u>phone</u>   <u>feather</u> <u>duster</u>   <u>short</u>-<u>cut</u>

- if the first word tells you what the second part is made of:

  <u>bread</u> <u>roll</u>   <u>plas</u>tic <u>bag</u>   <u>cheese</u> <u>cake</u>

- if the first part tells us the location of the second part:

  <u>city</u> <u>cen</u>tre   <u>back</u><u>door</u>   <u>garden</u> <u>path</u>

- if the new compound word is not a noun itself:

  <u>first</u>-<u>class</u>   <u>half</u> <u>price</u>   <u>second</u>-<u>hand</u>

Now try it!

191

Apply the rules you learnt above about stressing compound words, as you read these sentences.

Listen to the recording, and repeat.

1 The *troublemaker's fingerprints* were taken by the *overworked policeman*.

2 My *housemate* put her possessions into *cardboard boxes*, and carried them down the *staircase*.

3 She explained to her *granddaughter* that at *bedtime*, she had to get into the *single bed* and go to sleep.

4 They had to close the *airport* at *sunset* because there was a risk of *earthquakes*.

5 My mother made me a *wholesome* lunch, and put it in a *paper bag* for me to eat at *lunchtime*.

6 I've bought a *first-rate cell phone* to make business calls!

7 Is that a *brand new leather bag*, or was it *second-hand*?

8 Did she put a *first-class* stamp on that *home-made birthday* card she sent?

9 The *shopkeeper* doesn't accept *credit cards* if you're only buying a *newspaper*.

10 The *schoolchildren* were doing their *homework* in the *back row* of the *classroom*.

3 Suffixes can move the stress of the root word

192

The position of the stress changes in many root words when you add a suffix. Listen to these stress patterns.

- Some suffixes move the stress to the syllable before the suffix:

-ation	in<u>form</u>	infor<u>ma</u>tion
	re<u>pair</u>	repa<u>ra</u>tion
-ity	<u>mi</u>nor	mi<u>no</u>rity
	<u>real</u>	re<u>a</u>lity

- Other suffixes move the stress to another place in the word. You will have to learn these as you see them – they don't follow a rule.

  -ar   m<u>o</u>lecule   mol<u>e</u>cular

  -graphy   <u>ph</u>oto   phot<u>o</u>graphy

- Some suffixes take the stress themselves:

  -ade   <u>block</u>   block<u>ade</u>

  -ee   <u>em</u>ploy   employ<u>ee</u>

- Note that there are also a number of suffixes that do not affect the stress:

  -able   <u>fash</u>ion   <u>fash</u>ionable

  -ful   res<u>pect</u>   res<u>pect</u>ful

See Appendix 3 on page 145 for a full list of the most common suffixes and how they affect word stress.

Now try it!

193

Listen to the recording and try to hear all the stress patterns created by suffixes. How do they compare with their root word? Does the stress move?

1 The new *photography exhibition* by that *famous conceptual* artist only appeals to a *minority* of people.

2 There's so much *information* available about *ecology*, it's hard to know what's *official*.

3 Everyone was a bit *suspicious* of the *Democratic candidate*.

4 It's not difficult to find *volunteers* when you're training to be a *masseur*.

5 His scientific research into *robotics* made him a *millionaire*.

6 Don't *objectify* me, just because I'm *curvaceous* and *statuesque*!

7 The Indian countryside looks so *picturesque* during the *monsoon* season.

8 There was a *blockade* concealing the location of the *Japanese* embassy.

9 The *molecular biologist* was doing research into *atomic* particles.

10 If you've got a *suspicion* that there's something wrong with the wiring, call an *electrician* without *hesitation*!

Repeat the sentences, making sure that you stress the correct syllable in each word.

51

Sentence stress

At the end of Unit 48, we learned that English was a stress-timed language, and that one-syllable words can often become unstressed, along with the unstressed syllables of longer words, in order to give flow to a sentence.

He can have as many sandwiches as he likes, but it mustn't cost more than seven pounds fifty.

This means that these small, unimportant words disappear into an unstressed schwa sound.

The unimportant words are likely to be one-syllable grammar words like:

- *conjunctions:* and, but
- *prepositions:* on, in, at
- *articles:* a, an, the
- *pronouns:* he, she, it
- *auxiliary verbs:* have, has, do
- *forms of the verb 'to be':* is, am, was

These words are needed for the sentence to make grammatical sense, but they are not essential to the meaning of what is being said.

The important words will usually be:

- *verbs*
- *nouns*
- *adjectives*
- *adverbs*

194

Listen and pick out the most important words which carry the meaning of this sentence:

She was a huge fan of weekend breaks and usually tried to take a trip once a month.

Did you hear them?

- *verbs:* tried, take
- *nouns:* fan, weekend breaks, trip, month
- *adjectives:* huge
- *adverbs:* usually, once

If you were only given these words on their own, you would be able to work out what the sentence means from those words. If you were given only the unimportant words, (she, was, a, of, and, to, a, a), you would have no idea what the sentence was supposed to be about.

Now try it!

Here are the most prominent words from six sentences (we've added the pronoun so you know who we are talking about) but the words that have been reduced to schwas are represented as ----. Can you say the phrases?

1 (He) ---- climbed ---- hill ---- get ---- best view ---- ----city.

2 (They) ---- walked six kilometres ---- ---- rain just ---- get ---- ---- party. When ---- arrived ---- ---- soaked.

3 (She) ---- married ---- sailor. ---- went ---- sea ---- ---- never saw ---- again.

4 (he) All ---- cares about ---- money ---- power. ---- never remembers ---- parents' birthdays.

5 (She) ---- went ---- ---- races six times ---- year. ---- liked ---- gamble.

6 (he) ---- Wednesday, ---- shops were closed so ---- went online ---- got --- groceries delivered ---- next day.

Listen and compare.

Typical unstressed words

The table below shows some of the most common unimportant words which are often reduced to a schwa with sentence stress.

Articles

a / an	**the** (except before a vowel)
A glass of water.	Answer the phone.
He's an actor.	What's the time?
An officer and a gentleman.	The managing director.

Prepositions

for	**from**	**to**
What's for lunch?	She's from London.	Go to sleep.
Is that for me?	A letter from your father.	She gave that to her boss.
I'm lost for words.	It's a long way from here.	I'm going to the shop.
at	**of**	**than**
He works at the zoo.	The King of England.	Stronger than you.
Not at the moment.	Part of the solution.	Less than that.
The film starts at 7.30.	A glass of water.	More tired than yesterday.

Pronouns and determiners

there	**them**	**his / her**
There aren't any more.	Some of them got lost.	I've forgotten her name.
Is there a better way?	Show them the way out.	Ask her for help!
Is there much left?	I never liked them before.	She's his boss.
you	**some**	**that**
Are you coming or not?	Would you like some tea?	The way that we walked.
You won't believe this!	I wish I had some more.	The film that we saw.
Do you want me to call first?	I'll need some help.	The man that I loved.

Auxiliaries and smaller verbs

shall	have / has / had	was / were
What shall we do?	Where have you been?	I was confused.
We shall see about that?	We had waited all day.	We were late.
Shall I tell you the answer?	He has always known.	It was very dark.
do / does	**must**	**can**
Do you think so?	You must do as you're told.	What can I do to help?
What do you want?	They must work harder.	Can you speak Italian?
What does that say?	We must have forgotten.	She can be there tomorrow.

Conjunctions

as	and	but
He dressed as a pirate.	Fish and chips.	Naughty but nice.
Come as you are.	Good and evil.	I should try, but I won't.
We saw it as we went by.	Lost and found.	But you said you'd help!

Now try it!

196

Try reading the small phrases in the table, making sure that the unimportant words are turned into schwas. Listen to the audio to check that you are saying each one correctly.

! There are always exceptions. Sometimes the words in the table above are very important and carry the meaning of the sentence. At these times, they stay in their original form and are not pronounced as a schwa.

197

The obvious case is when you want to correct a misunderstanding.

– So you just want chips, right?

– Fish <u>and</u> chips, please.

Or, if you want to add particular emphasis.

– I'm looking for Michael.

– You've missed him, he literally *just* left.

But, these small words may also be stressed in natural speech as well. A typical example is when they are the last word in a sentence. For example:

– Where are you from?

or

– I'll buy some.

or

– I've got something better than that.

or

– I don't know if I can.

52

Combining the stresses

Knowing how to stress each word, and knowing which words are the most important in the sentence are both useful. But you need to be able to do both of these things at the same time to make a successful sentence. Here's how to go about building up word and sentence stress:

The talent was surprising.

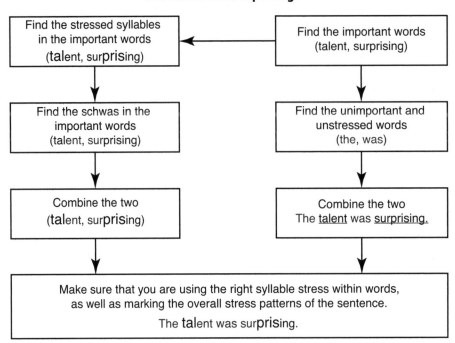

Now try it!

Look at the sentences. How do you imagine they would be spoken? Use the process above to work it out.

1   David had forgotten the other thing that he was supposed to do.

2   Libby was the life and soul of the party and everyone told her so!

3   Johanna was more excited than Tasha about the trip to Sweden.

4   Polly knew that her cream cake recipes were especially delicious and popular.

5   Becky loved to shop almost as much as Rachael loved computer games.

Now look at them written a different way to show how the stress and intonation work in the sentences.

- the most important words in the sentence are <u>underlined</u>
- the stressed syllables are in larger text
- the unstressed syllables (the schwas) are in grey
- and the rest of the text is in regular text

1 David had forgotten the <u>other</u> thing that he was supposed to do.

2 Libby was the <u>life</u> and soul of the party and everyone told her so!

3 <u>Johanna</u> was more excited than <u>Tasha</u> about the trip to Sweden.

4 Polly knew that her cream cake recipes were especially delicious and popular.

5 Becky loved to shop <u>almost</u> as much as Rachael loved computer games.

Listen and compare what you said to the audio.

Now try it!

Now let's try the stress in context. Again, decide for yourself which are the important and unimportant words. Record yourself, then listen back. Do you hear a clear balance of stressed and unstressed syllables?

> Hi Steve, I hope you haven't forgotten the party this evening. Just calling to give you the details. Come any time from eight, bring a bottle, and feel free to bring a friend or two. I sent you the address earlier, but it can be a bit difficult to find. So, when you come out of the station, turn left, and walk up the hill. It's quite a long road. After passing the park on your left, turn right into Scotland Street. My house is number twelve, with the bright orange door. The bell doesn't work, so you'll have to knock loudly. I've got no reception at home, so if you get lost, call my landline; you remember.
>
> Okay, see you later, and don't forget it's fancy dress!

Now, try reading the text below, with the stresses and schwas marked. Listen to the line-by-line audio. Did you have the same stress and intonation patterns that we had?

> Hi Steve, I hope you haven't forgotten the party this evening. Just calling to give you the details. Come any time from eight, bring a bottle, and feel free to bring a friend or two. I sent you the address earlier, but it can be a bit difficult to find. So, when you come out of the station, turn left, and walk up the hill – it's quite a long road. After passing the park on your left, turn right into Scotland Street. My house is number twelve, with the bright orange door. The bell doesn't work, so you'll have to knock loudly. I've got no reception at home, so if you get lost, call my landline; you remember.
>
> Okay, see you later, and don't forget it's fancy dress!

Listen again and mimic the stress patterns.

Finally, try and re-read from the unmarked copy of the text. Can you remember the stress patterns without the highlighting?

Practice exercises

Practice exercises

This section contains extra exercises for some of the sounds people usually find most challenging. First we will look at the difficult consonants and then the vowels.

Only attempt these exercises once you feel confident with the sounds themselves, otherwise this will be no fun at all! Go back to *Section B* if you feel you need a bit more practice.

The exercises start with tables which contrast the target sound with other similar sounds. Read across the lines of the table horizontally ➜ and listen for the contrast.

After that there are short stories or passages which allow you to put the sounds into practice. Make sure you recognize them all and sound them out, regardless of the spelling!

1 *th* sounds – /θ/ and /ð/

People often mix up the *th* sounds with either **/t/**, **/d/**, **/s/**, **/z/**, **/f/** or **/v/** sounds. In this exercise, you will have a chance to practise the contrast between *th* and all those sounds.

Read the lines of these tables horizontally, making sure that the consonants in each column sound really different from each other.

/t/ *and* /θ/ *sounds*

200

/t/		/θ/		/t/		/θ/
tick	➜	thick		true	➜	through
tanks	➜	thanks		boat	➜	both
taught	➜	thought		art	➜	bath
tie	➜	thigh		oat	➜	oath
tinker	➜	thinker		bet	➜	Beth
tin	➜	thin		tent	➜	tenth
heart	➜	hearth		tree	➜	three
tug	➜	thug		tum	➜	thumb
wit	➜	width		tread	➜	thread

/d/ *and* /ð/ *sounds*

201

/d/		/ð/		/d/		/ð/
doze	➜	those		dare	➜	there
dough	➜	though		breed	➜	breathe
den	➜	then		laid	➜	lathe
dine	➜	thine		seed	➜	seethe

(continued)

dare	➜	there		bad	➜	bathe
udder	➜	other		ride	➜	writhe
muddle	➜	mother		fodder	➜	father
Dan	➜	than		body	➜	bother
day	➜	they		ladder	➜	lather

/s/ *and* th *sounds*

202

/s/		th		/s/		th
boast	➜	both		moss	➜	moth
sigh	➜	thigh		certain	➜	thirteen
pass	➜	path		worse	➜	worth
sink	➜	think		saw	➜	thaw
say	➜	they		so	➜	though
sat	➜	that		mouse	➜	mouth
see	➜	three		sick	➜	thick
sort	➜	thought		sing	➜	thing
use	➜	youth		force	➜	fourth

/f/ *and* /v/ *and* th *sounds*

203

/f/		/θ/		/v/		/ð/
fear	➜	theory		clove	➜	clothe
fin	➜	thin		van	➜	than
phone	➜	throne		ever	➜	leather
oaf	➜	oath		lover	➜	loather
fawn	➜	thorn		fever	➜	feather
few	➜	through		mover	➜	mother
for	➜	thaw		over	➜	other
deaf	➜	death		vat	➜	that
fret	➜	threat		shaving	➜	scathing
fought	➜	thought		river	➜	rhythm

Read this email aloud, making sure that you pronounce all of the *th* sounds clearly.

204

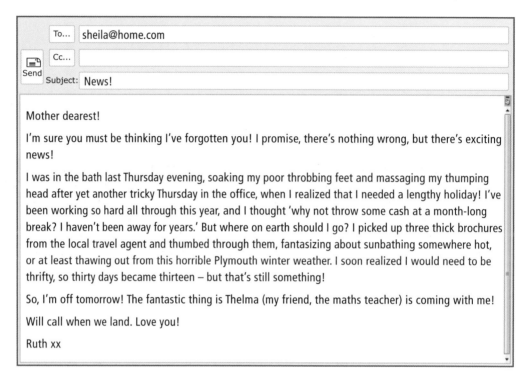

To...	sheila@home.com
Cc...	
Subject:	News!

Mother dearest!

I'm sure you must be thinking I've forgotten you! I promise, there's nothing wrong, but there's exciting news!

I was in the bath last Thursday evening, soaking my poor throbbing feet and massaging my thumping head after yet another tricky Thursday in the office, when I realized that I needed a lengthy holiday! I've been working so hard all through this year, and I thought 'why not throw some cash at a month-long break? I haven't been away for years.' But where on earth should I go? I picked up three thick brochures from the local travel agent and thumbed through them, fantasizing about sunbathing somewhere hot, or at least thawing out from this horrible Plymouth winter weather. I soon realized I would need to be thrifty, so thirty days became thirteen – but that's still something!

So, I'm off tomorrow! The fantastic thing is Thelma (my friend, the maths teacher) is coming with me!

Will call when we land. Love you!

Ruth xx

2 Light /l/ and dark /ɫ/ sounds

People very often mix up the dark and light *l* sounds.

Try reading the words in these tables, making sure that the two different sounds, the light /l/ and dark /ɫ/, are really different from each other.

205

light /l/		dark /ɫ/		light /l/		dark /ɫ/
low	→	pile	→	loud	→	all
allow	→	children	→	follow	→	help
friendly	→	adult	→	value	→	old
like	→	itself	→	actually	→	will
listen	→	fail	→	lesson	→	milk
hello	→	halt	→	later	→	spoil
slap	→	able	→	clean	→	sell
class	→	film	→	float	→	hall
lady	→	candle	→	flake	→	snail
let	→	ill	→	look	→	cool

Read this email aloud, making sure that you pronounce all of the *l* sounds clearly.

206

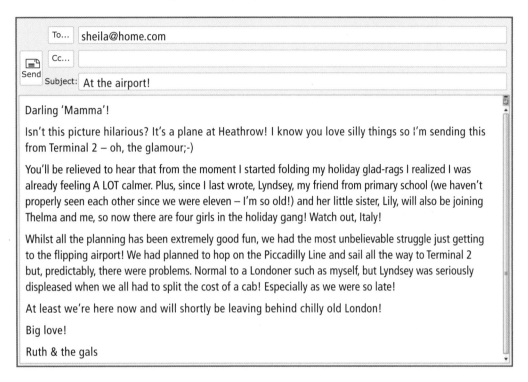

To...	sheila@home.com
Cc...	
Subject:	At the airport!

Darling 'Mamma'!

Isn't this picture hilarious? It's a plane at Heathrow! I know you love silly things so I'm sending this from Terminal 2 – oh, the glamour;-)

You'll be relieved to hear that from the moment I started folding my holiday glad-rags I realized I was already feeling A LOT calmer. Plus, since I last wrote, Lyndsey, my friend from primary school (we haven't properly seen each other since we were eleven – I'm so old!) and her little sister, Lily, will also be joining Thelma and me, so now there are four girls in the holiday gang! Watch out, Italy!

Whilst all the planning has been extremely good fun, we had the most unbelievable struggle just getting to the flipping airport! We had planned to hop on the Piccadilly Line and sail all the way to Terminal 2 but, predictably, there were problems. Normal to a Londoner such as myself, but Lyndsey was seriously displeased when we all had to split the cost of a cab! Especially as we were so late!

At least we're here now and will shortly be leaving behind chilly old London!

Big love!

Ruth & the gals

3 /ɹ/ sounds – initial, medial and final, and the silent *r*

The written *r* is generally only pronounced when it is followed by a vowel sound, and that may be in the initial position in a word or sometimes in the middle (medial) position. It is not pronounced at the end of a word unless it is a *linking* /ɹ/, joining up with a word beginning with a vowel sound, or an *intrusive r*, linking two vowel sounds. Look back at Unit 18 if you need to remind yourself of the rules.

Read the table horizontally, making sure that you pronounce the /ɹ/ sounds in the first two columns correctly, and that you *don't* pronounce any of the silent *rs* in the final two columns.

207

initial (spoken)		medial (spoken)		medial (silent)		final (silent)
red	→	arrive	→	shirt	→	car
really	→	around	→	nurse	→	more
right	→	trust	→	court	→	there
rock	→	create	→	marble	→	hear
rabbit	→	carrot	→	superb	→	star
road	→	original	→	fourteen	→	father
reason	→	Arabic	→	hurtful	→	never
wrong	→	horrible	→	large	→	lawyer
Rachel	→	brother	→	thirty	→	however

127

Read this email aloud, making sure that you pronounce all the *r* sounds clearly. Be careful that you don't pronounce any silent *r*s, and that you notice linking and intrusive *r*s.

208

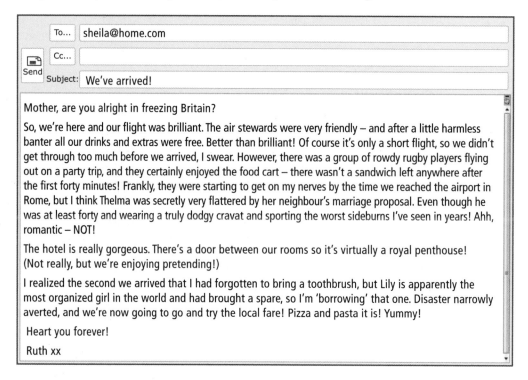

To... sheila@home.com

Cc...

Send Subject: We've arrived!

Mother, are you alright in freezing Britain?

So, we're here and our flight was brilliant. The air stewards were very friendly – and after a little harmless banter all our drinks and extras were free. Better than brilliant! Of course it's only a short flight, so we didn't get through too much before we arrived, I swear. However, there was a group of rowdy rugby players flying out on a party trip, and they certainly enjoyed the food cart – there wasn't a sandwich left anywhere after the first forty minutes! Frankly, they were starting to get on my nerves by the time we reached the airport in Rome, but I think Thelma was secretly very flattered by her neighbour's marriage proposal. Even though he was at least forty and wearing a truly dodgy cravat and sporting the worst sideburns I've seen in years! Ahh, romantic – NOT!

The hotel is really gorgeous. There's a door between our rooms so it's virtually a royal penthouse! (Not really, but we're enjoying pretending!)

I realized the second we arrived that I had forgotten to bring a toothbrush, but Lily is apparently the most organized girl in the world and had brought a spare, so I'm 'borrowing' that one. Disaster narrowly averted, and we're now going to go and try the local fare! Pizza and pasta it is! Yummy!

Heart you forever!

Ruth xx

4 /t/ and /d/

It is common to /t/ and /d/ sounds tricky. Read the lines of this table horizontally, making sure that you pronounce all of the /t/ and /d/ sounds accurately.

209

/t/		/d/		/t/		/d/
ten	➔	den		not	➔	nod
ton	➔	done		bet	➔	bed
bitter	➔	bidder		rot	➔	rod
writer	➔	rider		wrote	➔	rode
two	➔	do		hit	➔	hid
tour	➔	door		neat	➔	need
tear	➔	dare		height	➔	hide
utter	➔	udder		wheat	➔	weed
time	➔	dime		start	➔	starred
tie	➔	die		at	➔	add

Read this email aloud, making sure that you pronounce all of the /t/ and /d/ sounds clearly.

210

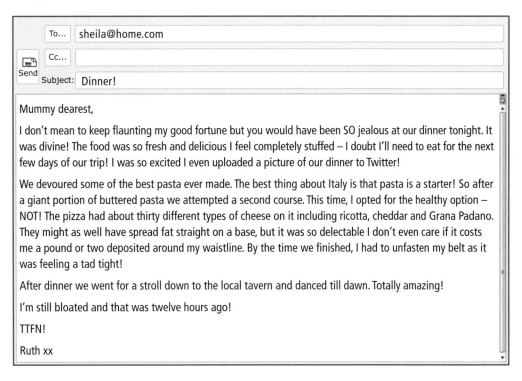

To...	sheila@home.com
Cc...	
Subject:	Dinner!

Mummy dearest,

I don't mean to keep flaunting my good fortune but you would have been SO jealous at our dinner tonight. It was divine! The food was so fresh and delicious I feel completely stuffed – I doubt I'll need to eat for the next few days of our trip! I was so excited I even uploaded a picture of our dinner to Twitter!

We devoured some of the best pasta ever made. The best thing about Italy is that pasta is a starter! So after a giant portion of buttered pasta we attempted a second course. This time, I opted for the healthy option – NOT! The pizza had about thirty different types of cheese on it including ricotta, cheddar and Grana Padano. They might as well have spread fat straight on a base, but it was so delectable I don't even care if it costs me a pound or two deposited around my waistline. By the time we finished, I had to unfasten my belt as it was feeling a tad tight!

After dinner we went for a stroll down to the local tavern and danced till dawn. Totally amazing!

I'm still bloated and that was twelve hours ago!

TTFN!

Ruth xx

5 /w/ and /v/

It is common to confuse /w/ and /v/. Read the lines of this table horizontally, making the consonant sounds in each column really different from each other.

211

/w/		/v/		/w/		/v/
wet	→	vet		wane	→	vane
wail	→	veil		waltz	→	vaults
west	→	vest		wiser	→	visor
wend	→	vend		wiper	→	viper
worse	→	verse		went	→	vent
wow	→	vow		will	→	evil
away	→	evade		aware	→	advise
rowing	→	roving		quota	→	voter
wary	→	vary		question	→	travel
wine	→	vine		wire	→	via

Read this email aloud, making sure that you pronounce all of the /w/ and /v/ sounds clearly.

212

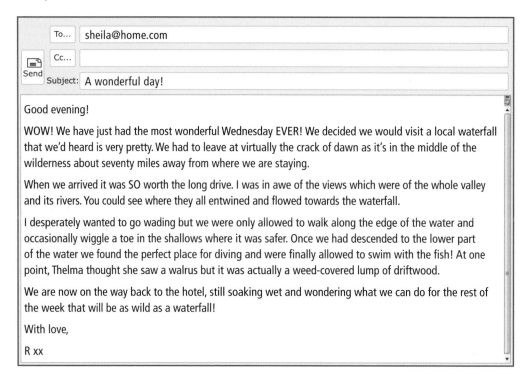

To... sheila@home.com

Cc...

Send

Subject: A wonderful day!

Good evening!

WOW! We have just had the most wonderful Wednesday EVER! We decided we would visit a local waterfall that we'd heard is very pretty. We had to leave at virtually the crack of dawn as it's in the middle of the wilderness about seventy miles away from where we are staying.

When we arrived it was SO worth the long drive. I was in awe of the views which were of the whole valley and its rivers. You could see where they all entwined and flowed towards the waterfall.

I desperately wanted to go wading but we were only allowed to walk along the edge of the water and occasionally wiggle a toe in the shallows where it was safer. Once we had descended to the lower part of the water we found the perfect place for diving and were finally allowed to swim with the fish! At one point, Thelma thought she saw a walrus but it was actually a weed-covered lump of driftwood.

We are now on the way back to the hotel, still soaking wet and wondering what we can do for the rest of the week that will be as wild as a waterfall!

With love,

R xx

6 /h/ sounds and the silent *h*

Sometimes an initial *h* is silent and people are often not sure when to say it and when not to. Try reading the lines of these tables horizontally, making sure that you pronounce all the /h/ sounds clearly when they should be pronounced.

213

initial (spoken)		medial (spoken)		initial (silent)
hat	→	ahead	→	hour
head	→	behave	→	honest
hot	→	reheat	→	heir
herb	→	unhelpful	→	honour
heavy	→	behind	→	heiress
heart	→	inhumane	→	hourly
home	→	behold	→	honourable
happy	→	inhale	→	honesty
hug	→	manhandle	→	honorary
who	→	forehead	→	hourglass

Read this email aloud, making sure that you pronounce all of the /h/ sounds, but not the silent ones!

214

To...	sheila@home.com
Cc...	

Send

Subject: Heatstroke!

Hiya!

We had a minor holiday hiccup today when Thelma decided to have a midday doze in 35 degree heat without a hat. Honestly! When she finally hauled herself off the beach and arrived back at the penthouse, she seemed to be hallucinating about having a husband who bred horses. I shouldn't have laughed but it was hilarious!

However, having realized something was really wrong we hurried her to the hospital, it was horrible – we had to manhandle her into a taxi with the help of the hotel staff. Thelma was NOT happy about that harsh treatment and got a bit huffy, even in her hazy state. Once we arrived at the hospital the doctor held his hand to her boiling hot forehead and immediately declared heatstroke. We had to wait for hours as they checked her heart and held her in for observation – we were hostages to her heatstroke!

Having been released, Thelma was very happy to get back to the hotel and as we were all hungry we headed out to dinner. Thelma had strict instructions to get some rest. However, this didn't hamper her mood as she was just so happy not to have a headache any more that she munched her hamburger whilst rehydrating on good old-fashioned H_2O.

Phew! Hope you had a better day!

R x

7 /s/ and /z/

It can be tricky to remember all the rules about pronouncing /s/ and /z/ sounds. Try reading the lines of these tables horizontally, making sure that the sounds in the /s/ column are all really different from the sounds in the /z/ column.

215

/s/		/z/		/s/		/z/
dice	→	dies		place	→	plays
race	→	rays		loose	→	lose
fuss	→	fuzz		spice	→	spies
grace	→	greys		course	→	cause
ice	→	eyes		close (adj.)	→	close (verb)
this	→	these		cease	→	seize
recent	→	reason		niece	→	knees
dose	→	doze		pace	→	pays
face	→	phase		house (noun)	→	house (verb)

Read this email aloud, making sure that you pronounce all of the /s/ and /z/ sounds clearly.

216

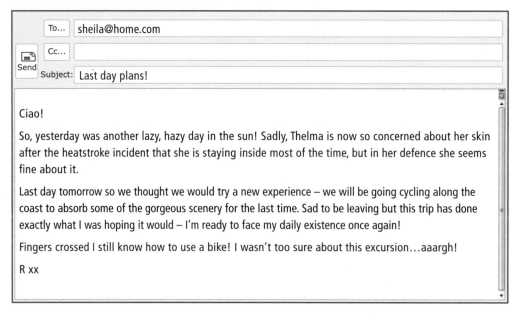

> To... sheila@home.com
>
> Cc...
>
> Send Subject: Last day plans!
>
> Ciao!
>
> So, yesterday was another lazy, hazy day in the sun! Sadly, Thelma is now so concerned about her skin after the heatstroke incident that she is staying inside most of the time, but in her defence she seems fine about it.
>
> Last day tomorrow so we thought we would try a new experience – we will be going cycling along the coast to absorb some of the gorgeous scenery for the last time. Sad to be leaving but this trip has done exactly what I was hoping it would – I'm ready to face my daily existence once again!
>
> Fingers crossed I still know how to use a bike! I wasn't too sure about this excursion…aaargh!
>
> R xx

8 /ŋ/

ng and nk are very common spellings for the /ŋ/ sound. In the case of ng, sometimes it is pronounced /ŋg/, and sometimes only as /ŋ/. Can you remember the rules? Go back to Unit 6 if you are not sure.

Read the lines of these tables horizontally, making sure that you use the pronunciation indicated.

217

/ŋg/		/ŋk/		/ŋ/
hunger	→	hunk	→	hang
anger	→	thank	→	gang
tangle	→	tank	→	tangy
shingle	→	sink	→	sing
finger	→	thinker	→	thing
longer	→	links	→	long
single	→	synchronize	→	slang
angle	→	anchor	→	rang
bangle	→	bank	→	bang

Read this email aloud, making sure that you pronounce all the right /ŋ/ sounds in the right places.

218

To...	sheila@home.com
Cc...	
Subject:	Coming home!

Hi Mum,

I know you'll think I'm going bonkers, but I just can't stop laughing about the events of the last two weeks. And in spite of breaking the bank to fund this trip, I still think it's the best thing I've done in ages! It was so great to hang out with a gang of girls and just spend some time doing my favourite things; sun-bathing, eating, laughing and RELAXING!

Really looking forward to seeing you next week. I think we're catching an early flight out because Lily hates flying at night, so I'll be popping in on my way home.

R xx

9 /ɪ/, /iː/ and /i/

The /ɪ/, as in KIT, the /iː/, as in SHEEP and the /i/, as in the final sound in HAPPY are very similar to each other. Try reading the lines of this table horizontally, making the differences between each column clear.

Remember that /ɪ/ is a short sound, and /iː/ is a long sound, made with the tongue a little higher than the /ɪ/. /i/ is a shorter /iː/ sound which comes at the end of a word.

219

/ɪ/		/iː/		/i/
lid	→	lead	→	literally
hid	→	heed	→	hippy
pitch	→	peach	→	pity
bid	→	bead	→	body
risen	→	reason	→	rosy
bin	→	been	→	beanie
is	→	ease	→	easy
slip	→	sleep	→	slippery
chip	→	cheap	→	cheaply
wit	→	wheat	→	witty
lip	→	leap	→	lippy
hit	→	heat	→	happy
Tim	→	team	→	tiny
ship	→	sheep	→	sheepishly
bit	→	beat	→	bitterly
dill	→	deal	→	doily
lick	→	leak	→	lucky
grid	→	greed	→	greedy
live	→	leave	→	lively
fill	→	feel	→	finally

10 /æ/ and /ɑː/

The /æ/, as in CAP, and the /ɑː/, as in BATH, are often confused. Read the lines of this table horizontally, making the differences between each column clear.

Remember that the /æ/ vowel is short and sharp, whereas words with the /ɑː/ sound all use the same long, open vowel sound. Be careful not to say any silent *r* sounds.

220

/æ/		/ɑː/		/æ/		/ɑː/
lap	→	laugh		mat	→	mark
active	→	article		mass	→	mask
scatty	→	scar		radical	→	rather
dank	→	dark		angry	→	after
attack	→	alarm		gas	→	gasp
hat	→	half		bat	→	bath
lack	→	lark		tan	→	task
back	→	bark		January	→	jar
hat	→	heart		back	→	basket
dalmatian	→	darling		cat	→	cart

11 /ɒ/, /ɔː/ and /əʊ/

The /ɒ/, as in LOT, the /ɔː/, as in THOUGHT, and the /əʊ/, as in GOAT, are often confused. Read the lines of this table horizontally, making the differences between each column clear.

Remember that /ɒ/, is a short vowel, whereas the /ɔː/ is a long vowel and /əʊ/ is a diphthong.

221

/ɒ/		/ɔː/		/əʊ/
hot	→	hawk	→	hope
lot	→	lawn	→	load
bond	→	bought	→	bone
shone	→	shorn	→	shown
pond	→	prawn	→	pony
wrong	→	raw	→	row
not	→	nought	→	note
cot	→	caught	→	coat
dot	→	daughter	→	don't
what	→	water	→	won't
dog	→	dawn	→	dopey
politics	→	port	→	pole
novice	→	naughty	→	notice
loss	→	laws	→	lows
honest	→	awful	→	owns
popular	→	paw	→	pope
mop	→	more	→	mope
costly	→	court	→	cosy
tonic	→	taught	→	tone
rot	→	raucous	→	wrote

12 /ʊ/ and /uː/

People often mix up the /ʊ/, as in FOOT, and the /uː/, as in GOOSE. Read the lines of this table horizontally, clearly sounding the different vowels.

Remember that /ʊ/ vowel is short, whereas the /uː/ is a long vowel sound.

222

/ʊ/		/uː/		/ʊ/		/uː/
foot	→	food		good	→	goose
hood	→	whose		should	→	shoes
woody	→	woozy		look	→	Luke
sugar	→	shoe		full	→	fool
pull	→	pool		pudding	→	poodle
cook	→	cool		butcher	→	boudoir
hook	→	hoover		wolf	→	wound
ambush	→	beauty		bullet	→	boot
rook	→	route		stood	→	stool
woman	→	human		crook	→	cruise

13 /æ/, /ʌ/ and /ɒ/

The /æ/, as in CAP, the /ʌ/, as in CUP, and /ɒ/, as in LOT, are often confused. Read the lines of this table horizontally, making the differences between each column clear.

These are all short vowel sounds. /æ/ is a front vowel, while /ʌ/ is made further back in the mouth, and the /ɒ/ vowel has lip rounding.

223

/æ/		/ʌ/		/ɒ/
trap	→	truck	→	trot
cap	→	cup	→	cot
pack	→	puppy	→	poppy
hack	→	hug	→	hob
slap	→	slug	→	stop
dad	→	duck	→	dock
apple	→	plum	→	orange
rapper	→	rubber	→	robber
batter	→	butter	→	bottle
haggle	→	hunter	→	toggle
whack	→	once	→	wash
bad	→	blood	→	body
fat	→	flood	→	foreign
swagger	→	swum	→	swan
bag	→	bus	→	box
add	→	udder	→	odd
hand	→	hundred	→	hobbit
cabbage	→	cupboard	→	cobble
plait	→	plug	→	plot
mat	→	mug	→	mop

14 /ɜː/ and /ə/

The /ɜː/, as in NURSE, and the /ə/, as in LETTER, are often confused. Read the lines of this table horizontally, making the differences between each column clear.

Remember that the NURSE words use a long vowel (with a silent *r*), and both COMMA and LETTER words end with the schwa. Be careful not to pronounce the *r* sound on the end of the LETTER words.

224

NURSE /ɜː/		LETTER /ə/		COMMA /ə/
nurse	→	neither	→	Nina
skirt	→	skier	→	Sarah
perfect	→	appear	→	Paula
work	→	whisper	→	wisteria
earth	→	either	→	area
journey	→	jeweller	→	Geneva
church	→	chancer	→	China
bird	→	bouncer	→	bacteria
certain	→	sister	→	samosa
early	→	earlier	→	arena
learn	→	lumbar	→	lava
courtesy	→	corner	→	comma
purple	→	potter	→	panda
stir	→	singer	→	salsa
version	→	visor	→	viva
worse	→	worker	→	Wilma
heard	→	hoover	→	hysteria
German	→	gangster	→	gorilla
earn	→	earner	→	idea
turn	→	tower	→	Tunisia

15 /e/ and /eɪ/

The /e/, as in DRESS, and the /eɪ/, as in FACE, are two more confusing sounds. The /e/ sound is short, while the /eɪ/ is a diphthong. Read across the table.

225

/e/		/eɪ/		/e/		/eɪ/
rest	→	race		met	→	mate
red	→	raid		neck	→	naked
led	→	laid		ten	→	attain
bread	→	braid		technology	→	taken
mess	→	mace		second	→	sake
beckon	→	bacon		edge	→	age
deaf	→	Dave		chess	→	chase
fell	→	fail		bet	→	bait
fed	→	fade		Jennifer	→	Jane
guess	→	gaze		get	→	gate

16 The sounds of the letter *a*

The job advert below demonstrates the different ways in which the letter *a* can be used in English spelling. Think about all of the pronunciations that can be required by the letter *a*. Try reading it aloud. Then, listen to the audio track to check if your pronunciation was correct.

226

This **a**dvert h**a**s been pl**a**ced in m**a**ny n**a**tional p**a**pers bec**au**se we **a**re pl**a**nning to **a**dd to our f**a**ntastic te**a**m of Chartered **A**ccount**a**nts.

After three triumph**a**nt dec**a**des, we h**a**ve est**a**blished **a** reput**a**tion **a**s **a** l**a**rge, **a**nd dyn**a**mic comp**a**ny, **a**nd we **a**re continuing to exp**a**nd. This is the ch**a**nce to g**ai**n experience in **a**ll **a**re**a**s of fin**a**ncial work.

Typic**a**l d**ai**ly **a**ctivities will include:

– M**a**n**a**gement of fin**a**ncial systems, **a**nd risk **a**nalysis.

– Undert**a**king l**a**rge-sc**a**le **a**udits of m**a**jor intern**a**tional comp**a**nies.

– Li**ai**sing with clients **a**nd **a**dvising on fin**a**ncial m**a**tters.

– Ev**a**lu**a**ting **a**nd testing fisc**a**l inform**a**tion.

– Giving **a**dvice on t**a**x**a**tion **a**nd **a**ssoci**a**ted tre**a**sury **a**ctivities.

– M**a**int**a**ining **a**ccounts **a**rchives.

– **A**dvising on business tr**a**ns**a**ctions, mergers **a**nd **a**cquisitions.

– Prep**a**ring fin**a**ncial st**a**tements, **a**nd **a**nnual **a**ccounts.

– Fin**a**ncial pl**a**nning **a**nd forec**a**sting.

The ide**a**l c**a**ndid**a**te will h**a**ve the following desir**a**ble **a**ttributes:

– **A** background in chartered **a**ccount**a**ncy.

– **A**n exempl**a**ry tr**a**ck-record.

– **A**n underst**a**nding of the d**ai**ly t**a**sks expl**ai**ned **a**bove.

– Outst**a**nding time m**a**n**a**gement.

– Consider**a**ble m**a**turity **a**nd the **a**bility to te**a**ch lower-r**a**nking trainees.

De**a**dline for **a**pplic**a**tions: 3rd J**a**nu**a**ry. Ple**a**se **a**ddress **a**ll **a**pplic**a**tions to the M**a**n**a**ging Director, Edw**a**rd Evering.

17 The sounds of the letter *e*

Now look at the letter below which demonstrates a variety of uses of the letter **e**. Read it aloud and then listen to the audio.

227

> D**e**ar **E**dward **Ev**ering,
>
> Having s**ee**n your adv**e**rt in this **ev**ening's pap**e**r, I am writing to **e**xpr**e**ss my int**e**r**e**st in the rol**e**.
>
> My **e**xp**e**ri**e**nc**e** in this fi**e**ld is **e**xt**e**nsiv**e** and th**e**r**e**for**e** mak**e**s m**e** the p**e**rf**e**ct p**e**rson to **e**nhanc**e** your **e**xisting t**e**am. I was **e**mploy**e**d for t**e**n y**e**ars at an **e**x**e**cutive l**e**v**e**l by **E**mily **E**sh**e**r Associat**e**s, in **C**entral **E**ss**e**x. My **e**v**e**ryday duti**e**s **e**ncompass**e**d **e**ach it**e**m on your d**e**tail**e**d sp**e**cification.
>
> I b**e**li**e**ve that I poss**e**ss all the n**e**c**e**ssary qualiti**e**s to b**e** **e**xtr**e**m**e**ly succ**e**ssful in your busin**e**ss, and it would b**e** a v**e**ry **e**xciting st**e**p in my car**ee**r. I hav**e** pr**e**viously b**ee**n r**e**sponsibl**e** for sup**e**rvising **e**ducation and int**e**rnship sch**e**m**e**s, and hav**e** **e**xc**e**ll**e**nt p**e**dagogical r**e**f**e**r**e**nc**e**s. I hav**e** also compl**e**t**e**d s**e**v**e**ral ind**e**p**e**nd**e**nt r**e**s**e**arch proj**e**cts into the b**e**st strat**e**gi**e**s for r**e**sourc**e** **e**nhanc**e**m**e**nt.
>
> If you d**e**cid**e** to invit**e** m**e** to int**e**rvi**e**w, I will b**e** **e**xtr**e**m**e**ly **e**xcit**e**d to d**e**monstrat**e** my **e**normous pot**e**ntial as an **e**mploy**ee**.
>
> V**e**ry b**e**st wish**e**s,
>
> Ian Pric**e**

18 The sounds of the letter *i*

The next letter demonstrates the circumstances in which the letter **i** can occur in English. Read it aloud and then listen to the audio track to check your pronunciation was correct.

228

> Dear Mister Price
>
> **I** liked your letter – **i**t was n**i**ce to hear that you th**i**nk so h**i**ghly of our **i**nstitut**i**on. F**i**rstly, we were **i**mpressed w**i**th the s**i**gnif**i**cant amount of **i**nformat**i**on you **i**ncluded **i**n your appl**i**cat**i**on. **I**n fact, we aren't conv**i**nced that th**i**s pos**i**tion **i**s su**i**ted to your **i**nd**i**v**i**dual sk**i**lls. After cons**i**derable d**i**scuss**i**on, we th**i**nk you m**i**ght benef**i**t from **i**ncreased respons**i**b**i**l**i**ty and the opportun**i**ty to bu**i**ld on your ex**i**sting exper**i**ence.
>
> Our **i**n**i**t**i**al **i**mpress**i**on **i**s that your qual**i**f**i**cat**i**ons make you an **i**deal cand**i**date for a higher level pos**i**tion w**i**th**i**n our **i**nstitut**i**on. **I**f you are **i**nterested **i**n the **i**dea of an execut**i**ve pos**i**tion, wh**i**ch would requ**i**re you to take on more superv**i**sory dut**i**es, we would l**i**ke to **i**nv**i**te you to **i**nterv**i**ew th**i**s week.
>
> Yours s**i**ncerely,
>
> Edward Ever**i**ng

19 The sounds of the letter *o*

This next letter offers examples of the letter **o** in English. Read it aloud before listening to the audio track.

229

Dear Mr Price,

I kn**o**w that it is n**o**t l**o**ng since y**o**ur interview, but we are writing t**o** inf**o**rm y**o**u that we th**o**ught y**o**ur perf**o**rmance was very str**o**ng, and y**o**u've g**o**t the j**o**b.

We were enc**o**uraged by y**o**ur **o**bvi**o**us c**o**nfidence with **o**nline meth**o**d**o**logies, and kn**o**wledge **o**f f**o**recasting pr**o**cedures. We h**o**pe that y**o**u will be able t**o** take resp**o**nsibility f**o**r **o**ur c**o**aching and ment**o**ring pr**o**grams f**o**r juni**o**r empl**o**yees. We are als**o** **o**ptimistic that y**o**u c**o**uld c**o**ntribute t**o** s**o**me **o**f **o**ur **o**ngoing c**o**rp**o**rate finance pr**o**jects.

This is a f**o**rmal **o**ffer **o**f empl**o**yment, and we are encl**o**sing c**o**mplete c**o**ntractual inf**o**rmati**o**n. Y**o**u are aut**o**matically eligible f**o**r **o**ur gener**o**us pensi**o**n plan, h**o**liday pay and numer**o**us **o**ther benefits.

Please inf**o**rm us sh**o**rtly as t**o** whether y**o**u w**o**uld be interested in c**o**ming **o**n b**o**ard. We h**o**pe y**o**u will ch**oo**se t**o** bec**o**me part **o**f **o**ur team, and l**oo**k f**o**rward t**o** welc**o**ming y**o**u t**o** the **o**ffice. We are **o**pen t**o** neg**o**tiati**o**n regarding when y**o**u will start with us – please c**o**mmunicate with **o**ur Human Res**o**urces **O**fficer, T**o**m C**o**urtney.

All being well, I l**oo**k f**o**rward t**o** w**o**rking with y**o**u very s**oo**n.

Best wishes,

Edward Evering

20 The sounds of the letter *u*

This email provides examples of the letter **u** in all of its possible English combinations. Read the passage aloud before listening to the audio track.

230

Dear S**u**san

I'm sorry I was o**u**t late again on Th**u**rsday and missed yo**u**r call. Yo**u** know that I wo**u**ldn't **u**s**u**ally spend so m**u**ch time at work. This job is j**u**st **u**nbelievably to**u**gh – I'm **u**nder a lot of press**u**re. There was bo**u**nd to be an adj**u**stment period, and I s**u**ppose it's **u**nderstandable that it feels da**u**nting at first. It's j**u**st s**u**ch a great b**u**siness to be part of, tho**u**gh. I feel so **u**tterly pro**u**d that they tho**u**ght I was good eno**u**gh, and I j**u**st want to make a s**u**ccess of it.

My team seem a nice b**u**nch; they're h**u**gely q**u**alified, and **u**ndo**u**btedly **u**nderstand their d**u**ties thoro**u**ghly. I j**u**st hope that I can **u**nite them more, and enco**u**rage them to p**u**t a bit more f**u**n into their work. At the moment they're all a bit st**u**ffy and **u**n**u**s**u**ally **u**ptight for s**u**ch a yo**u**ng gro**u**p of people.

Anyway, I m**u**stn't gr**u**mble, beca**u**se I'm really very l**u**cky! I've got a s**u**perb job that stim**u**lates me. I can pict**u**re myself staying here for a long time, if they let me – and if yo**u** like it here too, of co**u**rse (and I j**u**st know yo**u** will). So I sho**u**ld really get back to work. I am very l**u**cky to have s**u**ch a wonderful, **u**nderstanding wife and I can't wait to have yo**u** here with me in the new ho**u**se, starting o**u**r new life. I g**u**arantee yo**u** a h**u**ge h**u**g when yo**u** get here at the weekend, and a fab**u**lo**u**s life here soon!

All my love,

Ian

Section F

Appendices

Appendix 1 Spelling patterns of unstressed sounds

/ə/ The tables below show the most common spelling patterns of the unstressed schwa sound.

-er /ə/	-ion /ən/	con- /ən/ com- /əm/	-or /ə/	-ous /əs/
lawyer	information	container	doctor	fabulous
singer	station	convincing	director	glamorous
teacher	occasion	computer	Windsor	marvellous
brother	migration	compassion	actor	scandalous
sister	dedication	commit	author	curious
mother	socialization	combine	sailor	anxious
father	nation	comedian	raptor	boisterous
power	region	command	minor	cautious
mower	location	conniving	mirror	curvaceous
heather	hesitation	commence	sector	disastrous

-land /lənd/	-mouth /məθ/ -ton /tən/	-urgh /ə/ -ough /ə/	-ford /fəd/	-ham /əm/
Scotland	Plymouth	Middlesbrough	Oxford	Nottingham
England	Bournemouth	Edinburgh	Stamford	Bellingham
Ireland	Portsmouth	Loughborough	Stratford	Cheltenham
Iceland	Kensington		Watford	Fulham
Finland	Boston			Graham
dockland	Dalton			gingham

-ate /ət/	-our /ə/	pro- /pɹə/	-ment /mənt/	a- /ə/
delicate	harbour	produce (vb)	commitment	allow
intricate	candour	pronounce	excitement	abort
elaborate	labour	provide	enjoyment	annoy
fortunate	ardour	prolong	government	attend
laminate	favour	promiscuous	development	adore
separate	saviour	project	investment	arrange
celibate	colour	proclaim	employment	afford
passionate	ardour	procession	argument	again
disparate	demeanour	probation	management	about

-graphy /gɹəfi/	for- /fə/	-a /ə/	to- /tə/	-logy /lədʒi/
choreography	forgot	India	tomorrow	ecology
photography	forgetful	China	today	biology
cinematography	forgive	Canada	tonight	archaeology
geography	forever	Russia		anthology
biography	forbid	gorilla		astrology
bibliography	forlorn	banana		chronology
orthography		Helena		dermatology
videography		ultra		genealogy
radiography		panda		psychology
		comma		apology

-ar /ə/	-al /əɬ/	-acy /əsi/	su- /sə/	-ian /ən/ or /iən/
molecular	local	bureaucracy	supply	guardian
polar	historical	democracy	submit	mathematician
beggar	contextual	aristocracy	submerge	bohemian
burglar	intellectual	accuracy	success	historian
calendar	loyal	celibacy	succumb	civilian

caterpillar	paternal	delicacy	subtract	comedian
cheddar	bacterial	privacy	subscribe	custodian
cougar	pedal	pharmacy	subsist	librarian
dollar	penal	surrogacy	succeed	civilian
hangar	ritual	intimacy	suppose	comedian

The evolving /ə/

This is an example of the evolution of the spoken word. Some speakers say these words with a SCHWA and others use a weak form of the KIT vowel. The words in the table below use a weak form of KIT rather than the /ə/.

pre- /pɹə/	*be-* /bə/	*de-* /də/	*re-* /ɹə/
predict	believe	decide	report
preserve	beneath	deduce	require
prefer	below	delight	reduce
pretend	bedeck	delicious	receive
prevent	begin	define	relief
present (vb)	behind	derogatory	respect
prepare	bewitch	deny	reveal
prerogative	before	desist	respond
prescription	between	detect	remove
presenter	betrothed	defend	recite

/ɪ/ Some words use a different weak form to the schwa – an /ɪ/. The purpose of using this sound is exactly the same as the schwa: to create contrasting stress. In the table below, the use of /ɪ/ is more typical of all speakers.

-age /ɪdʒ/	*-es* /ɪz/	*ex-* /ɪg/ or /ɪk/	*-ed* /ɪd/	*e-* /ɪ/
average	roses	example	wanted	eternal
mileage	surprises	explode	decided	elated
vintage	poses	excite	wasted	emotion
advantage	closes	explain	folded	erratic
hostage	faces	explore	debated	erase
drainage	places	exasperate	related	efface
shortage	chases	expose	recorded	emote
dosage	races	expire	excited	enrage
postage	choices	extend	started	envelop (vb)
marriage	places	expect	abducted	ensue

ne- /nɪ/ *se-* /sɪ/	*-ice* /ɪs/ *-ace* /ɪs/	*-in* /ɪn/	*-et* /ɪt/	*-edge* /ɪdʒ/ *-ege* /ɪdʒ/
negotiate	justice	virgin	rocket	knowledge
neglect	notice	origin	pocket	college
negate	novice	coffin	locket	
Nepal	apprentice	vitamin	poppet	
seduce	avarice	melanin	socket	
secure	chalice	admin	closet	
second (vb)	cowardice	penicillin	jacket	
severe	prejudice	toxin	market	
secluded	solace	bargain	banquet	
secrete (vb)	surface	boffin	basket	

Appendix 2   The spoken and the silent *r* – a quick guide

In Unit 18 you learnt that many written *r*s are not pronounced. You also learnt that an /ɹ/ is sometimes pronounced when it is not written – when it is a linking or intrusive /ɹ/.

The table below will give you more practice in the different instances of the spoken and silent /ɹ/.

the spoken /ɹ/	the silent *r*	the linking /ɹ/	the intrusive /ɹ/
If you see an *r* before a vowel sound, it is spoken.	If you see an *r* before a consonant or a pause in speech, it is silent.	If you see an *r* between two vowel sounds, it is spoken. ❗Remember: vowel *sounds*, not vowel spellings.	When /ɔː/ or /ə/ are followed by another vowel sound, an /ɹ/ sound is added. ❗Remember: vowel *sounds*, not vowel spellings.
rat	car	here‿and now	media/ɹ/event
really	cart	four‿hours	law/ɹ/and order
rattle	pardon	car‿and bike	vodka/ɹ/and tonic
rake	party	they'‿re on top	visa/ɹ/or debit
react	star	sure‿I can	saw/ɹ/a bird
create	third	pair‿of shoes	India/ɹ/and China
crab	thirty	jar‿of jam	Sarah/ɹ/and Helen
great	shirt	however‿it is	schwa/ɹ/and intonation
trap	concert	whenever‿I can	idea/ɹ/of it
tragedy	starting	there‿isn't time	panda/ɹ/in the zoo
arrow	vicar	Doctor‿of music	claw/ɹ/ing
arrogant	courteous	manager‿of the band	draw/ɹ/ing
Eric	journalist	wander‿around	Joanna/ɹ/is often late
brother	dirty	sister‿-in-law	Eva/ɹ/isn't here
bring	earth	star‿of the show	Marina/ɹ/is a star
break	forty	bizarre‿antics	India/ɹ/is hot
trade	international	stir‿it all in	car/ɹ/in the garage
string	heard	over‿and out	thaw/ɹ/ing out
irritate	burnt	four‿and a half	Canada/ɹ/is pretty
carry	fire	letter‿or card	the gorilla/ɹ/is big
hero	stirred	never‿again	the area/ɹ/over there
trade	stored	further‿away	comma/ɹ/in the sentence
carrot	bored	sugar‿and spice	the diva/ɹ/of the night
tyrant	born	Professor‿of law	ultra/ɹ/absorbent
tragedy	Bournemouth	actor‿and model	banana/ɹ/and custard
foreign	Oxford	utter‿idiot	drama/ɹ/on stage
borrower	poor	major‿issue	America/ɹ/or Canada
Florida	ignore	core‿exercises	the pasta/ɹ/is delicious
horrible	core	power‿on	vanilla/ɹ/or chocolate
glamorous	power	ignore‿it	data/ɹ/entry
staggering	lowered	Vicar‿of Dibley	his camera/ɹ/is expensive
wondering	lawyer	store‿it in the loft	the tiara/ɹ/is gorgeous
veronica	Norway	fire‿at the aliens	the agenda/ɹ/is too full
bride	important	door‿on the left	his paranoia/ɹ/is funny
carry	virtuous	this chair‿is comfy	this drama/ɹ/isn't over
stereo	smart	over‿and over	
		after‿a while	

Appendix 3   Suffixes and word stress

It's important to remember that suffixes can affect word stress. Below you will find some of the most common examples, but always bear in mind that no rule is rigid, and there are exceptions to any pattern.

The following suffixes, when added to a root with two or more syllables, will move the stress to the syllable before the suffix. So, when the root is only one syllable, it will be on that one syllable.

suffix	examples
-ion	procession, recognition, television, cancellation, amplification
-eous	curvaceous, courageous, righteous advantageous, erroneous, instantaneous
-ic / -tic	atomic, heroic, acidic, robotic, athletic
-ical	methodical, alphabetic, analytical, grammatical, symmetrical
-ial	official, commercial, colonial, controversial, territorial.
-ian	beautician, politician, historian, musician, librarian.
-ity	minority, authority, security, activity, responsibility
-cracy	democracy, bureaucracy, aristocracy, autocracy, meritocracy
-ual	conceptual, intellectual, contractual, residual, contextual
-ious	suspicious, mysterious, victorious, luxurious, fictitious

The following suffixes when added to a root with two or more syllables will move the stress to the syllable two syllables before the suffix.

-graph	-crat	-ate (adjectives)	-ar	-ise / -ize
photograph	bureaucrat	delicate	spectacular	supervise
autograph	democrat	articulate	popular	criticize
telegraph	aristocrat	ultimate	bipolar	emphasize

The following suffixes will be stressed themselves.

suffix	examples
-ade	blockade, arcade, invade, biodegrade, lemonade
-eur / -euse	masseur, chanteur, chauffeur, connoisseur, entrepreneur
-air(e)	millionaire, billionaire, questionnaire, extraordinaire, legionnaire
-ee / -eer	employee, jamboree, pedigree, volunteer, mountaineer, puppeteer, auctioneer
-ette	vinaigrette, marionette, baguette, cassette, cigarette
-ese	Chinese, Japanese, legalese, obese, Maltese
-ique / -esque	physique, boutique, antique, statuesque, burlesque, arabesque, picturesque
-oon	monsoon, balloon, afternoon, tycoon, cartoon

Some suffixes don't affect stress, and the way the root is stressed doesn't change when the suffix is added.

suffix	examples
-ish	foolish, devilish, childish, amateurish, feverish
-ism	racism, atheism, capitalism, elitism, narcissism
-ist	pianist, alarmist, cyclist, illusionist, lyricist
-ment	development, movement, management, employment, argument
-ful	stressful, beautiful, delightful, respectful, powerful
-able	acceptable, adaptable, knowledgeable, agreeable, fashionable
-less	breathless, bottomless, expressionless, meaningless, speechless
-ary –ery -ory	infirmary, stationary, imaginary, bribery, contradictory

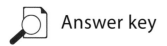

Answer key

Unit 18

The giant pand<u>a 'i</u>s definitely our favourite animal. We love their⌢ amazing faces, and black and white colouring. Pandas are⌢extremely fond of eating bamboo, and you'll often find them with their pa<u>w 'o</u>n a bamboo plant! Unfortunately, the pand<u>a 'i</u>s an endangered species, which means there⌢aren't as many of them around as there used to be. You're⌢unlikely ever to see a pand<u>a'</u> in the wild – in order to do that, you'd have to become an explorer⌢and travel to Chin<u>a 'o</u>n holiday. Chin<u>a 'i</u>s the only country where⌢any pandas live outside captivity. And you won't find them in every are<u>a 'o</u>f Chin<u>a 'a</u>s they're⌢only in Western areas. I wonder⌢if I'd have to arrange a vis<u>a 'i</u>n order to go to China. I'm sure⌢it'd be worth it!

Unit 43

1   He was so gorgeous! ↑

2   She was being ridiculous. ↓

3   It was a really hard exam. ↑

4   He was wearing such hideous shoes. ↓

5   I'm too tired for this. ↑

6   I'll only be a few minutes. ↑

Unit 47

ghost (1), waiter (2), organize (3), unhappiness (4), pronunciation (5)

one syllable	two syllables	three syllables
house	paper	fantastic
big	language	syllable
truth	increase	argument
through	parking	prominent
	weaker	

four syllables	five syllables
reality	undeniable
authority	indiscriminate
education	monosyllabic
observation	

2   very – has two syllables and the others have one

3   participation – has five syllables and the others have four

4   computer – has three syllables and the others have two

5   opposition – has four syllables and the others have five

6   unexpected – has four syllables and the others have three

Unit 48

China   surprise   for<u>g</u>et   visa   sta<u>ti</u>on

foc<u>us</u>   spe<u>c</u>ial   <u>ob</u>ject   re<u>g</u>ard   be<u>s</u>ide

Unit 49

1

a-	be-	com-	con-
allow	believe	computer	container
again	begin	complain	convince
about	because	commit	condition
de-	for-	pre-	pro-
decide	forget	predict	pronounce
delicious	forgive	present	professional
demand	forbid	prepare	provide
re-	su-	to-	o-
report	supply	today	occur
regret	support	tomorrow	occasion
respect	surprise	tonight	observe

2

-er	-or	-our	-ar
lawyer	doctor	harbour	polar
teacher	professor	favour	sugar
leader	director	colour	dollar
-a	-ous	-ate	-logy/-graphy
India	fabulous	delicate	biology
China	anxious	separate	apology
panda	curious	intricate	photography
-ion	-acy	-ment	-al
information	democracy	government	local
complication	privacy	commitment	historical
occasion	accuracy	excitement	tribal
-ton	-ford	-land	-ham
Kensington	Oxford	England	Birmingham
Boston	Watford	Scotland	Graham
Dalston	Stratford	Iceland	Fulham

Note to teachers

This book can be used for self-study, but will work equally well in a classroom situation when used by pronunciation or EFL teachers. As accent coaches, we would encourage all EFL teachers to embrace the teaching of pronunciation in the classroom – and we aim to make your life as easy as possible by providing you with material that can be manipulated to work in any classroom environment.

It is important to approach pronunciation systematically. The learning process is not just something that happens in the brain – it is muscular so changes don't necessarily happen quickly. They require a lot of repetition to become instinctive. We recommend focusing on one sound, or a pair of sounds, at a time, allowing the student(s) to become fully confident with each sound before introducing the next sound shift. Otherwise the process can very quickly become overwhelming and demoralizing for learner and teacher alike! Because speech sounds are repeated throughout speech, even one sound shift can yield big results. We would advise covering one rule per class – that way you won't need to give up the whole lesson to pronunciation but you will still see results with every single lesson. Or, if time allows, devoting a whole class to cover a couple of bigger, trickier rules will offer more impressive results.

Don't feel the need to work through this book from start to finish – the units are all self-contained and can all stand independently. The layout is broadly based on the order we use to structure our own courses (consonants first, then monophthongs, and diphthongs, before moving on to connected speech) but you should feel free to work in whatever order makes most sense for you and your learners. Don't forget the additional online material available for further practice of the trickiest sounds!

Section D of this book is dedicated to the rhythm of RP – the stress and intonation patterns of English that, when mastered, will enable speakers immediately to sound more natural when they speak. We would urge you not to underestimate the importance of this section when teaching pronunciation. Even the most fluent students will gain from a glance over these units.

If you speak with a different regional accent from the standard southern English (RP) accent that we teach in this book, feel free to teach the sounds that apply in your area. You can still use our tables and word lists – just model your own sound in class, rather than using the audio and video. Geography is as good a reason as any to teach a different sound system, and in many instances may be a more logical decision than sticking rigidly to RP. As long as you are clear with your students about what they are learning, and you are both happy with the decision, so are we! Alternatively, if you want to teach modern RP, but it's not your native accent, we recommend using the video clips and audio tracks in your lessons to demonstrate the sounds.

Lastly, please trust your own ears above the 'language groups' icons (see page iii for more information on these). These are designed to be broad guidelines for self-study to cover every possibility. It's very likely that individual students will vary hugely – not doing some of the things we say they will, and doing additional things that we haven't mentioned. This is normal, because our accents are constantly changing and evolving. The best thing to do is to work with what you hear, and be specific about your adjustments.

What next?

Now that you have finished this book you will understand, in theory, what you need to do to change your accent. However, this is only one part of the process. Remember, changing your accent takes time and, more importantly, it takes practice.

Learning an accent is like learning any new physical skill – for example learning to dance. Reading a book about the theory and history of ballet will not make you a ballet dancer. To become a skilled dancer, you need to put in the time practising the steps and developing your strength. Learning a new accent is exactly the same – as well as learning the theory and the rules you need to establish the muscle memory so that your tongue and lips have the flexibility and strength to produce the new sounds whenever you need them.

This means that the process of changing your accent can feel very frustrating, because you now know what you need to do to produce a sound, but it just isn't happening; the muscles simply don't understand what you are asking them to do. When you feel like this, remember that even knowing that you're making a mistake means that you have learned something! So if you are *aware* that you are mispronouncing your 'r' sounds every time you make them, you are already making progress, even if it doesn't feel like it!

What are the best ways to practise?

Clients often tell us 'now that you've told me, I'll never make that mistake again. I'll get it right every time.' Experience has shown that this is not a realistic expectation. In high-pressure situations, just finding the right words is hard enough without also worrying about which sounds you're using to say those words.

The best way to improve pronunciation is to work systematically by giving yourself small, manageable tasks and focusing on specific sounds. For example:

- Select a paragraph from a newspaper or magazine. Read it aloud, focusing purely on pronunciation, not on meaning.
- Select several common words that give you an opportunity to practise something you're working on and try to pronounce them correctly every time. For example, if you're working on *th*, try to say it right every time you say 'Thank you'.
- Set yourself short tasks such as ordering in a restaurant, recording a voicemail message, or asking for directions while focusing on pronunciation.
- Record yourself and listen back – that way you will be able to reflect objectively on your progress.

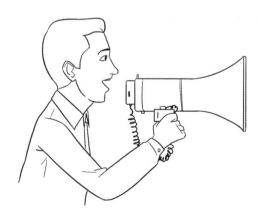

Then relax! Enjoy communicating, and don't worry about pronunciation. Every week, gradually build up the length of time that you practise for. This way, you are more likely to *want* to practise, to work with awareness, and build new habits gradually, rather than driving yourself crazy, and giving up. This is a gradual process, which will take time.

Make your practice count

When you find a word that you find really difficult, don't ignore it! We find that people often rush over the sounds and words they find most difficult to pronounce. Sometimes people try to avoid certain words altogether!

Your most challenging sounds might be frustrating to work on, but they will also be so rewarding to get right!

You need to work slowly and meticulously, breaking the tricky sentences down into small individual sections that you can perfect and then gradually build back up, so that your articulators are able to make all of the necessary shapes.

Start by finding the sound you find most difficult in the word or phrase:

Say the sound ➜ add a sound before/after ➜ practise a word ➜ practise a sentence

For example, the word 'hungry':

ng /ŋ/ ➜ ung ➜ hungry ➜ I'm not hungry any more.

If you're finding it hard to make progress

We recommend investing in some one-to-one sessions with an accent coach to help you identify what is holding you back. Make sure that you choose someone with recognized qualifications, and whose approach you trust.

Your coach will be able to act as an impartial set of ears to check your work, and give you honest feedback on what you're doing well, and what you need to do in order to improve.

Above all, don't give up! Enjoy the process of improving each sound, and give yourself credit for the progress you make. Keep your old recordings – in years to come, you might just enjoy listening to how far you've come!

Good luck!

Sarah & Helen

Glossary

1 Mobile and fixed articulators

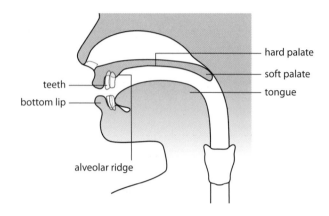

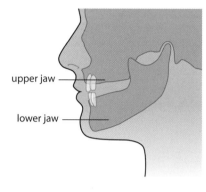

2 Tongue

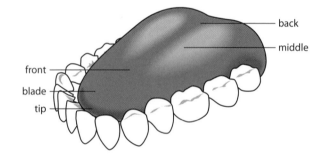

3 Teeth

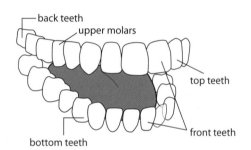

4 Lip movements

widen your lips / wide lips

part your lips

lips are neutral/relaxed

round your lips/rounded lips

seal your lips

assimilation	a feature of connected speech where one sound changes to become more like the sound next to it
consonant	a sound you make by restricting the airflow with a combination of your fixed and mobile articulators
consonant cluster	a group of consonant sounds pronounced together (like *str* or *fths*)
diphthong	a vowel sound made of two vowel components, made by moving your articulators
evolving	of something that is changing over time
falling tone	an intonation pattern which ends lower than it started
fluent	of speech without pause or errors
glottal stop	a plosive consonant sound where the air is stopped by the vocal folds in the larynx (the IPA symbol is /ʔ/
hiss	a long sound made by letting air out through a very restricted space
intonation	the tune of your speech, the combination of different rising and falling tones used in a sentence
lisp	a very common speech defect, affecting the pronunciation of /s/
loan word	a word taken from another language (English has many loan words, such as 'bungalow' and 'bangle' from Indian languages, or 'cafeteria' from Spanish)
monophthong	a pure vowel sound made without any movement of the tongue or other articulators
monotone	of speech which has no variation in pitch
nasal sound	a consonant made by a complete obstruction of air as it passes through the vocal tract and is then suddenly released
native language	your own language; the language you learned as a child
onglide	of the sound you make moving into a new mouth position
pitch	describes the highness or lowness of a tone (in the case, that we are speaking on)
plosive consonant	a consonant made by a complete obstruction of air as it passes through the vocal tract and is then suddenly released
prefix	a letter or group of letters added to the beginning of a word to make a new word, like *re-*, or *pre-* or *sur*
rising tone	a voice pitch which ends up higher than it started
schwa	a short, voiced vowel sound made with all the articulators in a neutral, relaxed position (it is the most common sound in the English language and the IPA symbol is /ə/)
stress	a letter or group of letters added to the end of a word to make a new word, like *-tion*, *-ful*
suffix	the emphasis put on a word or syllable when you say it
sustainable sound	a sound that can be continued at the same level
syllable	a sound in speech that usually contains one vowel sound (it can be a word or part of a word)
vocal folds	the small muscles inside the larynx which vibrate to turn air into voiced sound
voiced	of a sound for which the vocal folds are vibrating, including all vowel and some consonant sounds
voiceless	of a sound for which the vocal folds are not vibrating
vowel	a voiced sound you make with an open mouth and without using your mobile articulators to stop the airflow
whisper	sounds or words which are voiceless, using only the breath, without vibration from the vocal folds
word boundary	where one word meets another
yawn	the action of opening your mouth very wide to take in a lot of air; we do this when we are tired

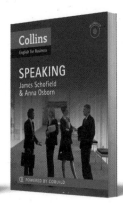

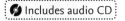
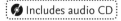

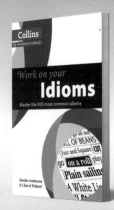